GAMES *for* GIRL SCOUTS

THIRD EDITION

D1230905

Girl Scouts of the U.S.A.
420 Fifth Avenue
New York, N.Y. 10018

GIRL SCOUTS OF THE U.S.A.®

Betty F. Pilsbury, *President*
Mary Rose Main, *National Executive Director*

Inquiries related to *Games for Girl Scouts* should be directed to Program, Girl Scouts of the U.S.A., 420 Fifth Avenue, New York, N.Y. 10018

Credits

Project Coordinator	Chris Bergerson
Contributor	Audrey Major
Illustrator	Eleanor Kwei
Design	Antler & Baldwin Design Group

Printed in the United States of America
ISBN 0-8841-347-0
15 14 13 12 11 10

CONTENTS

INTRODUCTION

This is a third, and major, revision of *Games for Girl Scouts*. In revising it, we have tried to include games that are Girl Scout favorites, as well as formalize some of the game activities that Girl Scouts are involved in across the country, such as wide games and nature awareness games. We have also included a section on program links and an annotated Bibliography that should assist in further exploration of games. We have greatly expanded the selection, almost doubling the number of games. We hope that all who use this book will enjoy many wonderful times with games in Girl Scouting.

CHAPTER 1

GETTING STARTED

WHY GAMES?

Games have been a part of Girl Scouting since Juliette Gordon Low, the founder of Girl Scouting, rewrote the original handbook, *How Girls Can Help Their Country,* in 1916. In Girl Scouting, games are an opportunity for developing group cooperation, teamwork, and self-confidence. The games found in this book and in other Girl Scout books (see pages 115–118, "Girl Scout Program Links") provide opportunities for fun, exploration of interests, skill development, leadership, and learning.

Play and games are a part of every adult and child's growth experience. Through games we transmit cultural values and develop social and physical skills. Participation in games can contribute to physical, mental, and emotional fitness. Through a positive game environment, girls can learn and practice rules of fair play, develop self-control and self-awareness, and learn to win or lose graciously. Games provide girls with an opportunity to share their knowledge and experiences through participation, as well as an opportunity to evaluate their experiences.

Games also provide a vehicle to creatively explore cultural values and important issues such as pluralism, sexual stereotypes, competition, cultural differences, and an understanding of disabilities.

COMPETITION AND COOPERATION: NOT AN EITHER/OR SITUATION

There are several schools of thought on the kinds of games that are appropriate for children. Recent movements advocate noncompetitive games for all ages, with particular emphasis on forming noncompetitive and cooperative values that will carry over to real-life situations.

As previously noted, games often reflect the values of a society. They also provide an opportunity to shape those values. Competition is viewed as an integral part of American society; it is commonplace in business, social, and sports situations. The ability to be competitive is greatly respected if it is a competition infused with fair play and sportsmanship. Winning at all cost is no longer acceptable in today's society. Today, there is an increasingly global economy, linked across borders by economic, environmental, and social concerns. Cooperative and teamwork skills are needed in all aspects of society, including competitive situations.

Through Girl Scouting, the leader of games can strive to create the proper environment for learning the skills and developing the attitudes needed for cooperation, teamwork, and competition. Girl Scouting, as an all-girl organization, enables girls to develop leadership skills and other skills that are often difficult to achieve in co-educational environments. Women in today's society are at a disadvantage if they have not learned how to compete, particularly in the working world. Girls can feel comfortable in trying different things in safe environments and have fun, too. Losing should not be equated with failure if games afford opportunities for fun and learning. Winning can build an appreciation for competition, teamwork, and leadership skills.

Here are some things to consider when playing games:

1. Emphasize fair play and cooperation in game-playing. Teamwork is important in group play, for each person contributes to the success of the total group.

2. Many traditional games, including games found in this book, can be modified to fit the needs of the group. This includes de-emphasizing competition, adapting a game to rotate girls back into play rather than have them "out" on the sidelines, and making sure that each team finishes with the help of the whole group.

3. Good sportsmanship is more than following rules. It involves attitude, fairness, equity, and the willingness to cooperate to have a successful experience for everyone.

4. Winning is desirable when competing, as it can add excitement and drive to a game, but girls need to learn to win and lose graciously. Competition is unhealthy when winning becomes the sole purpose of playing.

5. Failure should never be viewed as defeat. It should happen in a loving and accepting environment, and offer the opportunity for learning and developing different strategies in future games. However, a girl and the group should have the option of quitting or moving on to something else.

6. Do not underrate evaluation in game-playing. Take time to discuss how the game has been played, what has been learned, how the girls feel about the way they interacted, and any changes that need to be made. Talk about the issues of fair play and sportsmanship as they arise, and give everyone an opportunity to voice her opinion and be a part of the group decision.

BEING FLEXIBLE, CREATIVE, AND SENSITIVE TO GIRLS' NEEDS IN GAME-PLAYING

Making adaptations in game-playing can teach valuable lessons in creativity, initiative, compromise, and flexibility. Most games can be adapted for different age groups, the mood of the group, the skill of the players, and to emphasize the cooperative aspects of the competition. Changes can be made to take into consideration group size, the playing area, or a day of inclement weather. A large group can be broken down into smaller groups when small group participation is needed.

Games can also be adapted to specific needs and themes. For example, girls' names can be used in a game to make it an introductory game; or an indoor game might be changed to a nature game by moving it outdoors.

A group might also create a totally new game. Many games are based on actions such as running, hopping, hiding, passing something, guessing, or sitting or standing in a circle or a line. Challenge girls to invent their own game with at least two of these actions contained within the game. Let them determine whether they want to emphasize skill, competition, cooperation, or all three.

Be aware of games that might offend or be interpreted differently by some group, or games that promote stereotypes. Just as with all Girl Scout program, it is necessary to be sensitive to issues of pluralism and inclusion. Religious holiday themes in games or wide games have the potential to exclude members of different religions and should not be used. Games that promote sexual or racial stereotypes through actions or words also should not be used. Games that leave girls out because of language, dress, or disabilities should not be promoted. Avoid games that use or waste food or natural resources. Be sensitive to games that emphasize social status or use expensive materials or equipment. It is very important that a leader be able to communicate these concerns to girls when assisting them in their game selection, or when problems arise.

Learn how girls with different cultural backgrounds view competition, as well as how physical contact, such as hugging and touching, eye contact or lack of eye contact, and flexibility with rules, are handled.

Playing games is and can be part of the acculturization process for immigrants or girls with different cultural backgrounds. Different points of view should be respected and girls should not be forced into situations that make them uncomfortable. When cultural differences arise, or the need for sensitivity is anticipated, it is best to talk with everyone who may be involved. This may or may not include the total group.

GAME LEADERSHIP: ADULT AND GIRL ROLES

Throughout this book there are references to the "leader" or the "game leader." Frequently, with younger girls, the game leader is the adult Girl Scout leader or her assistant in the troop or group setting. Often, the game leader is selected from among the troop or group members. This might be a rotating duty for patrols or someone drawn from an "it or other" bag during the meeting. Sometimes the game leader for a Brownie or Junior Girl Scout troop may be an older Girl Scout, such as a program aide or someone working on her Girl Scout Silver or Gold Award.

Picking a game leader can be a fun game in itself. Ways to select a leader can be found on pages 22–23 in Chapter Two.

The role of the adult in planning and leading games will depend upon the girls' ages, their social development, the length of time the adult has been working with them, and the type of game being chosen and introduced.

Just as with all Girl Scout program, the girl-adult partnership should be an underlying principle in determining the game leader's role. Girls should be involved in:

- the selection of the game to be played.
- refereeing and determining the rules.
- dealing with group dynamics, equity, teamwork, competition, and evaluation of games.
- teaching games.
- the planning and running of game events.

As girls have more opportunities for leadership, the adult's role as the game leader should lessen. The adult role should become that of a facilitator and observer as girls work at developing their game leadership skills. Provide a structure that helps girls use the creative process. The structure may include stipulations regarding the following: purpose, number of players, motor skills, format, age appropriateness, scoring, equipment, rules, and boundaries.

Use girl-adult partnership in helping to select games appropriate for the group size and age range. Start out with high-activity games that get the group moving.

The adult facilitator should give girls an opportunity to determine the course of the game and deal with problems as they arise. As girls grow older, they can take more responsibility for safety, rules, and social issues, provided they are given the groundwork upon which to make decisions and act on their values.

Girls should be able to talk about the games afterward. Getting their reactions to the games and suggestions for adaptations is a part of the learning process.

An adult may find herself as a participant in a game, adding to the enthusiasm and providing a role model for the group. However, there are times when it might be better to play the role of observer or facilitator and not participate in a game.

Leading games can develop social and leadership skills in girls. Girls can learn informally within the group, or participate in a game leadership workshop. The latter is encouraged for older girls who are working with younger girls on a regular basis. A troop, group, or workshop environment can provide a safe and supportive environment for learning. It is important that girls be given the opportunity to practice and refine their skills if they are to become game leaders.

ON CHOOSING SIDES AND GIVING EVERYONE A CHANCE TO PLAY

When choosing up sides, make sure that you use a variety of methods to ensure different combinations of girls and distribution of the experienced and inexperienced. Chapter Two includes some helpful games and hints for dividing groups.

When playing competitive games, try to make teams even in skill and experience level. Avoid situations where girls are chosen for popularity or skill at the expense of the unpopular or unskilled. Girls of any age can be devastated if they are chosen last. As an adult leader or game leader you can work with the troop to put the emphasis on inclusion and teamwork, rather than exclusion or ranking. Girls need to learn to respect each others' strengths and weaknesses as a part of teamwork.

Rotate leadership so that all girls have an opportunity to experience the role. Balance the kinds of games that you play, so that different girls have opportunities to excel.

Try to play games so that people are not left out or eliminated. Change games so that people can come back into the game instead of sitting on the sideline. If the object is for one girl to win all, you do not always need to play to the "bitter end" while the others look on. However, there are times when elimination games are fine.

HOW TO LEAD GAMES

A good game leader needs to know how:

to **L**augh

to be **E**nthusiastic

to be **A**ctive

to be **D**emocratic

to be **E**ncouraging

to **R**espect each group member

The following tips may be used by game leaders. Teaching games is as easy as:

GET READY . . .

An important function of the leader is to get a group going without dragging out the explanation and game preparation. Here are some timesaving tips:

1. Review the health and safety checklist on pages 14–15 to help in the selection of a game for your group.

2. Understand the rules yourself before you present the game to others (you might jot down the key points of the game on an index card and keep it in your pocket).

3. Have any necessary equipment on hand.

4. Establish any necessary boundaries that will be used during play.

5. Anticipate and eliminate safety hazards in the playing area.

6. Have a plan for getting teams or formations organized quickly.

GET SET . . .

Capture the attention of your group. Here are some ways to get and keep group attention when starting out:

1. Use the Girl Scout quiet sign. Wait for silence. It is important to command the respect of the group by not attempting to talk over others.

2. Ask everyone to form a circle. Start off the circle yourself by taking the hand of two girls and enlisting their aid to gather the rest of the group.

3. Use another game or song to lead into your game, such as the song "One Elephant Went Out to Play" or a mixer such as birthday lineup (see page 19).

4. Use alternating loud and soft speech, unusual or unexpected facial expressions, or body movements.

5. Use a whistle. This can be effective with very large groups when necessary, but can be overdone, particularly if indoors.

GO! . . .

1. Give the name of the game and state its purpose. If you know the origin of the game, or anything of special interest about it, share that as well.

2. Describe the game briefly, giving the basic rules. It is usually easier to explain a game when standing or sitting in a circle with a group. In this way everyone can see and hear you, and you can immediately respond to a raised hand, a question, or a puzzled look. (If the game is to be played in teams, you may want to organize the teams first and have them stand together.)

3. Sometimes it may help to demonstrate the game with a small group of girls.

4. Ask for questions before you start to play.

5. Have clear-cut start and finish lines.

6. Have the group agree to follow the rules that are outlined in the directions given, or decide the rules beforehand. It helps to have written rules or a referee in some games. The group can change or make up rules as they play, if the group has agreed to do this beforehand in order to make the game better.

7. Decide, with the group, on a definite starting signal. This might be, "Ready, set, (pause) go!" or "On your mark, get set, go!" If the game is a relay, be sure that the girls know how each succeeding player is to start.

8. During rest periods, explain procedures again, if necessary, and let the group suggest ways to improve the game if needed.

9. Stop when enthusiasm is still high. (But make sure that everyone has had a chance to be "it" who wanted to be.)

ADAPTATIONS FOR SPECIAL NEEDS

Games and activities can be adapted to meet the special needs of girls with disabilities. In working with a group with a range of ability, a leader should be aware that *all* girls have abilities that fall somewhere on a continuum. These include:

1. Learning. The ability to understand new ideas and to master new skills.

2. Communication. The ability to read, understand and convey ideas through speaking and writing.

3. Motor and physical ability. The ability to move about, use tools, and manipulate objects.

4. Emotional adjustment. The ability to accept personal strengths and weaknesses and to react to situations in a socially appropriate manner.

5. Sensory ability. The ability to hear, feel, see, speak, and taste.

A group may contain girls who are low on one or more of the continuums because of different rates of physical or social development, lack of experience, or because of a specific disability or combination of disabilities. For more information, see *Focus on Ability: A Leaders' Guide to Serving Girls with Disabilities.* The following are some guidelines for leaders and girls in working with girls with disabilities:

1. Discuss a girl's special needs with her parents, teacher, and, in some instances, her physician if you have questions regarding limitations for specific activities. (This is particularly important if the girl is an ongoing member of a troop.)

2. In some cases, it is a good idea to prepare the rest of the girls in your troop for a girl with a specific disability. This would include talking about how you might adapt activities for this girl, how the girl can be included in all activities, and when to offer help. When the girl is introduced, she should not be labeled as the one with the disability, but discussion of her disability should not be avoided if it is brought up. In other cases, such as with a mild disability, an adult or game leader needs to see how the girl functions within the group before deciding whether to address the group. It may not be necessary.

3. The focus should be on what a girl can do, not what she cannot do. A girl will generally indicate what she is able to do for herself. Often, an adult or the group will want to do too much for the girl with a disability, which can take away any benefits of the experience for the girl.

4. Health and safety are prime considerations for activity and site selection, particularly when working with girls with disabilities. Know ahead of time any special needs (such as medications, bathroom assistance) or physical limitations of equipment (such as wheelchairs, braces, breathing apparatus).

5. When choosing a game, ask:

- Can all girls participate in the game as it is currently played?
- If all girls cannot participate in or be successful in all or in part of the game, what part needs adaptation? (It is much better to have partial participation than no participation.)
- Can the girl herself or the group come up with ways to adapt the game?

HEALTH AND SAFETY CONSIDERATIONS

Health and safety considerations should be the primary determination of the games played and the sites chosen. The following is a checklist for planning games and game events to ensure health and safety:

Choosing the game

- Is the game age-appropriate?
- Is the game within the players' experience or skill level?
- Is the game appropriate for the physical condition of the players?
- Is the game appropriate for indoors or outdoors?
- Is all game equipment checked out beforehand?

Choosing the playing area

- Is there room enough for the game?
- Has the playing area been checked out? Are there any hazards in or near the playing area? Can they be eliminated? If not, can safe play occur around them?

- If an active game is planned for indoors, is proper ventilation available? Are girls dressed appropriately?
- Does the site meet *Safety-Wise* standards recommended for meeting places and playing sites?
- Is drinking water available? Is a restroom available nearby?

During the game

- Are there a first aider and a first-aid kit available?
- Is the adult or game leader watching for signs of overheating and overexertion? Is the play prolonged beyond the capabilities of the players? Does the group take water and rest breaks?
- Is proper safety gear being used?
- Are girls who are outdoors dressed properly for the weather? Do they wear sunscreen, when needed?
- Is there a referee or game leader to oversee the safety and rules of fair play for all players, or are there ground rules laid ahead of play?

HOW TO USE THIS BOOK

This book is arranged under easy-to-reference chapter headings. See pages 123–128 for an Index of games by name and activity type.

Symbols appear next to each game, when appropriate. The categories are as follows:

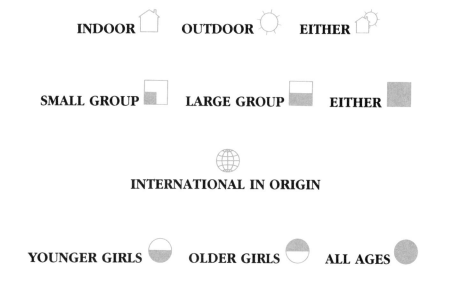

INDOOR   **OUTDOOR**   **EITHER**

SMALL GROUP   **LARGE GROUP**   **EITHER**

INTERNATIONAL IN ORIGIN

YOUNGER GIRLS   **OLDER GIRLS**   **ALL AGES**

It should be noted that these categories are only meant as guidelines. The sections "Adaptations for Special Needs" and "Health and Safety Considerations" in this chapter will be of further help.

CHAPTER 2

GETTING-TO-KNOW-YOU GAMES

INTRODUCTION GAMES

Found Object

How to play: Each girl uses something she has found in a room, in her purse, or outdoors to introduce herself to the group. It should be an object that tells something about herself. Set a time limit for the search. Have the girls form a circle and give each girl an opportunity to introduce herself and her object.

Getting Acquainted

How to play: Form a circle with one girl in the middle. A minute is given for each girl to learn the names of the girls on her left and right. The girl in the center of the circle points to someone and says "left" or "right." The girl indicated must call out the name of her neighbor before the one in the center counts to ten. If a girl cannot do it, the group calls out the name and she changes places with the girl in the middle.

Variation: After the one-minute learning period, a ball or beanbag is passed around the circle as music is played. When the music stops, the girl holding the ball or beanbag tries to name the girl on her right or left. If she doesn't remember the name, the entire group calls it out, and the game continues.

How Many Names?

You need: A pencil, a sheet of paper, a slip of paper for each girl, and safety pins or masking tape.

How to play: Each girl writes her name on a slip of paper. This slip of paper is pinned on her back. On signal, each girl tries to read the names on the backs of other girls while trying to keep them from reading her name. She writes the names she succeeds in reading on her sheet of paper while the game is in progress. When the leader calls "time," the girl with the most names wins.

Linda Lemon

How to play: Girls make a circle. Tell the girls they are going to the market to purchase something they like, but it must begin with the same letter as their first name. The first girl might say, "My name is Linda, and I am going to the store to buy a lemon." The next girl might say, "My name is Malia, and I am going to the store to get a mango *and* a lemon." Player three might say, "My name is Naomi, and I am going to the store to buy a nightshirt *and* a mango *and* a lemon." The last girl gets to name everything!

Variation: Play shopping bag upset. Have the girls change places and repeat the process from any place in the circle.

My Name Is

How to play: Girls sit in a circle or a number of small circles, depending upon the size of the group. One girl is asked to tell the group her name. She says, "My name is Kelly Green." The girl on her left then says, "Her name is Kelly Green and my name is Maria Lopez." The next girl then says, "Her name is Kelly Green, her name is Maria Lopez, and my name is Shanna Smith." This continues until the last girl in the circle tries to name all the girls in the group. If a girl cannot recall a name, others in the circle may help her.

Thumbnail Sketch

How to play: Each girl chooses a partner. During a three-minute period, they try to learn five things about each other by asking and answering questions such as these: "Where are you from?" "What is your interest in Girl Scouting?" "Do you have pets?" "What is the most fun thing you have ever done?" "What is your name?" Each girl then presents a thumbnail sketch of the girl she has just met.

Toss the String

You need: A ball of string or yarn. Groups of 15 or less.

How to play: Have the group form one or more circles. The girl with the ball of yarn starts by calling out a girl's name and tossing the yarn to her, being sure to hold onto the end of the string. The girl who catches the ball must call out another girl's name and toss the ball to her. The object is to include everyone and create a spiderweb with the string. The leader can then ask one girl to pull on her string while everyone else holds on. How many girls can feel the string being pulled? Use this as a starting point for a discussion on the importance of group cooperation and an individual's contribution to the group.

Where Are You From?

You need: Unobstructed space and girls from diverse geographic areas (such as at a state or national event). Mark the playing area North, South, East, and West with cards or arrows.

How to play: Instruct the girls that they are to place themselves in the playing area that corresponds to where they are from. After the group have decided their placement, have each girl introduce herself to the total group, with her name and a slogan about where she is from. For example, "My name is Katie and I'm from Missouri, the 'Show-Me' state."

WARM-UP GAMES AND MIXERS

Birthday Lineup

You need: An area where girls can line up.

How to play: Explain to the group that you want them to line up in chronological order, according to birthdays, without talking. After the girls have lined up, discuss how they arrived at their formation and note if there are any double birthdays.

Chain Puzzle Game

How to play: One girl is "it." She turns her back to the group. The other girls form a chain by clasping hands with the girl in front and behind. The game leader then leads the chain in and out under the girls' hands into any position possible without dropping hands. "It" is called on to untangle the chain without breaking the links.

Human Knots

How to play: Five to ten girls stand in a circle. Each places her hands in the center and takes hold of the hands of two people other than those standing next to her. The group must work together to untie the knot without releasing hands.

Invention Game

You need: Preassembled bags of assorted items for each group. Items might include straws, rubber bands, paper clips, spools, pencils, clay, or clothespins.

How to play. Give each group a bag of items. Ask them to invent such things as playground equipment or a machine that has a specific function, such as to help with a household job or to carry objects. Have each group share its invention with the total group when completed.

Nosebag Skits

You need: Preassembled bags of assorted objects and clothing that can be used in a skit. Kitchens are a good source for such objects.

How to play: Divide the group into teams. Each team is given a bag with an item for each girl in it. The group is given five to ten minutes to create a skit using all of the items.

Word Makers

You need: Cards with individual letters of the alphabet printed on them. If the group is large, add extra vowels. Avoid q, x, and z.

How to play: Give each girl a card. Ask the group to form words of three to four letters. The game leader should recognize the groupings formed and then signal and have individuals find other groupings.

Variation: The group with the longest word wins.

Yes or No

You need: Buttons or peanuts, ten per player.

How to play: Each girl is given ten peanuts or buttons. The girls ask each other questions about the things they are interested in. Each girl attempts to make her opponent answer "yes" or "no." If a girl answers with either word, a peanut or button is forfeited to the inquirer. At the end of the game the girl having the largest number of peanuts or buttons wins.

DIVIDING-UP-THE-GROUP GAMES

These are games that can be used to divide groups up when teams or relay groups are needed.

 *Number Call Out*

How to play: Assemble the group. Call out a number such as "three" and the girls must scramble to get in groups of three. Try for numbers that divide evenly into your total group, or have those left out be the next callers.

Variation: Girls must get into combinations that do not include people from previous combinations.

Ice Cream Flavors

How to play: Have girls silently choose chocolate or strawberry ice cream as their flavor. They are not to tell anyone of their decision. Everyone then closes her eyes and calls out the flavor she selected. Girls continue to call out their flavor while seeking others with the same flavor to come and join hands. The game ends when everyone has found her flavor. If the teams are uneven, ask someone to voluntarily move to the other team.

Just Like Me

How to play: The game leader calls out things that girls might have in common, such as ponytails, an older sister, a piece of red clothing, the same height, and so on. On signal, everyone must quickly get into groups that have the common characteristic. Be careful not to use racial, cultural, or sexual stereotypes in dividing into groups. If the groups are uneven, have one group join another.

Variations: Make groups by month or date of birth, initials of the first or last name, favorite school subject, or completion of the same Try-It, badge, or interest project.

Leg Extension

How to play: Have everyone stand in a circle. On the count of three each girl must extend one leg into the circle. All right-legged girls become a group and all left-legged girls become another group.

 *Fingers Up*

How to play: Instruct all girls to hold any number of fingers up in the air. All those with a matching number of fingers become a team, or all odd numbers and all even numbers become a team.

 *Odd/Even*

How to play: As girls line up, each is given an odd or even number. They must then form two groups based on odd and even numbers.

SOME WAYS TO SELECT GAME LEADERS

 *Number Guess*

How to play: Ask a patrol leader, or someone who is not involved in the game, to write a number on a piece of paper. Have each girl try to guess the number. The one whose guess is the closest will be the leader.

 *It/Other Bag*

You need: Two paper bags and a slip of paper for each girl.

How to play: Label two bags "it" and "other." Put the names of all the girls in the "it" bag and pick a name from that bag to select a leader. When the game is over, put that name in the "other" bag. When a new "it" is needed, pick again from the "it" bag.

 *Colored Paper*

You need: A paper bag and equal numbers of two different colors of slips of construction paper for each player, plus a slip that is a different color.

How to play: Place equal numbers of strips of two colors of construction paper (for example, blue and red) plus one strip of a different color (for example, white) in a paper bag. Each girl draws a slip of paper and the girl who draws the odd strip is the leader.

 *Jan-Ken-Po*

This Japanese game is a version of the traditional rock-paper-scissor-stone game.

How to play: To start, two or more girls close their fists and swing them in a downward movement while saying "jan-ken-po." On the third downward motion they show a frog (scissors), snake (paper), or slug (stone). Repeat the downward motions while saying "ai kono sho." Girls can make the same or different hand motions. The frog can chop the snake, or the snake can bite the slug, or the slug can slime the frog. Girls are eliminated after each round of play until one person remains and becomes the leader.

 *Counting Rhymes*

How to play: Use counting rhymes such as the one that follows, while pointing to a different girl as each word is said.

"Two, four, six, eight,
Who do we appreciate?
G-I-R-L S-C-O-U-T-S"
The girl the last letter in "Girl Scouts" falls on is out. The game continues until only one girl is left to become the leader.

Create your own counting rhymes for more fun. Avoid any rhymes that might be insensitive to race or ethnicity.

CHAPTER 3

QUIET GAMES FOR INDOORS OR OUTDOORS

ACTING GAMES

 *Animal Who Am I?*

How to play: Divide the girls into groups of five to ten. Tell them that they must form their groups into types of animals or insects. Give each group time to work together. Then everyone tries to guess what animal or insect each group is.

 *Art Tableau*[1]

You need: A variety of pictures showing people in action. They can be clippings from magazines or prints of famous paintings.

How to play: Divide the group into teams of five to eight girls each. Place the pictures around the room and let the girls inspect them briefly. The pictures are then collected and one is given to each team. The team must invent a skit or dialogue based on the situation in the picture. Allow approximately two minutes for each presentation, but give the group longer for preparation.

Variation: Each team is given one picture with five to eight people in it. They look at it closely for a few minutes. Then they turn it over and try to arrange themselves in the positions shown in the picture or try to describe what each person in the picture is doing.

Emotional Charades

You need: A watch that times seconds; prepared slips of paper, one per girl, that have a phrase describing an emotion and age level. For example: "angry child," "happy baby," "sad teenager," "hungry middle-ager."

How to play: Divide the group into two teams. Each team rotates in sending one girl to the game leader. Each girl selects a slip of paper and acts out her phrase for *her* team. Her team has two minutes to guess the phrase. The team having the fastest time for guessing all the phrases is the winner.

Variation: Each team can compose a list of words and topics for the other team to act out and guess—for example, movie, song, or book titles. Place the words in a bag for each team. Each girl draws a word or phrase and acts it out for her team. Keep track of the time it takes for each team to

---

[1]From *200 Games for Guides,* by Maureen Price. Brown, Son & Ferguson Ltd., Glasgow, Scotland. Copyright 1964. Reprinted with permission of the publisher.

guess the word or phrase. At the end of play, the winning team is the one with the fastest time.

 *Fashion Show*

You need: Newspapers and tape for each group. Crayons or markers can also be used.

How to play: Divide girls into partners or teams, with materials for each team. Each partner or team chooses a model. The object is to create an outfit for each model. The results can be judged in terms of speed, creativity, or amount of covering.

GUESSING GAMES

 *Artists*

You need: Paper and markers, pens, or crayons.

How to play: The group is divided into teams of about five to eight players. Each team is numbered off and given a crayon or marker or pen. On signal, all No. 1 players, the "artists," run to the game leader, who whispers the name of an object each must draw and gives each one a piece of paper. On signal, the girls run back to their teams and immediately begin to draw. Team members try to guess the object. When they guess correctly, the artist runs back to the leader. The first team to send its artist back to the leader wins a point. The No. 2 players of each team then become the artists and the game proceeds. Simple objects such as a house, cat, or tree can be used with younger girls and progressively more complex things or ideas can be used for older girls.

Variations: Have the girls draw book, movie, or song titles, or simple sayings; or have each artist stand in a line with her hands behind her back and face the group. The game leader hands the first artist something, which she passes to the next artist, who keeps it behind her back while feeling it but not seeing it. While passing the object, the game leader must be sure it cannot be seen by the other players. When all artists have felt the object, they are given crayons and paper. Each artist runs back to her team and draws a picture of the object. Team members try to guess the object drawn by their artist.

Baby Pictures

You need: A numbered baby pict[...]
for each player.

How to play: The pictures are pl[...]
number. Girls write down the numbe[...]
signal, each girl tries to identify as m[...]
within a specified time, putting names [...]

Find the Leader

You need: Someone to designate a leader.

How to play: The group sits in a circle. "It" goes out of the room or away from the group, and a leader is designated. The leader leads the group in a series of motions, such as hand-waving, foot-stomping, and ear-wiggling. "It" returns to the center of the circle, as the group is following the leader, and must guess who the leader is. When "it" guesses correctly, the leader then becomes "it."

Introductions

You need: Slips of paper, each with a different sentence written on it.

How to play: Two girls are selected. The first one leaves the room while the second girl memorizes a sentence. (For example: "Look before you leap.") She then leaves the room while the first girl comes in to memorize an entirely different sentence. (For example: "It was my grandmother's old recipe.") The second girl is called in again and someone else introduces the two as "Ms. Garcia and Ms. Smith, who are both interested in photography." (Their interest can be any subject—for example, space exploration or wildlife safaris.)

The two selected girls must talk together; the first one to bring her sentence into the conversation naturally and sensibly, after three opening remarks, wins the game. Two other girls are selected and the game continues. The winner of each game introduces the next two girls.

You need: A demonstration lattice made from four or more sticks, approximately 15 inches long, for each team; a variety of small objects for each team; a scarf or paper to cover the lattice.

How to play: A demonstration lattice of sticks is laid out on the ground with an object, such as an acorn, a maple leaf, or a feather, placed in each opening. Teams are formed. All teams observe the completed lattice for one minute before it is covered up. Each team then makes one of its own, trying to remember each object and its correct placement. The team constructing the most accurate lattice in the shortest time wins. (The objects used by the teams for their own lattices may be provided by the game leader or gathered by each team.) This game may also be played indoors. See page 91 for a WAGGGS variation.

Musical Guesswork

You need: Small items such as a star, an apple, a horse, a bell, a toy boat, a baseball, a Girl Scout book, or pictures.

How to play: Form two or more teams of three to eight players. The teams sit or stand together, all facing the game leader. The game leader takes one of the items from a box or bag and shows it to the entire group. Each team tries to think of a song title about the item or containing the name of the item. The first team to sing a line from a song related to that item scores one point. Here are some songs that the items might suggest:

"When You Wish Upon a **Star**"
"Don't Sit Under the **Apple** Tree"
"Horsey, **Horsey**"
"Jingle **Bells**"
"Row, Row, Row Your **Boat**"
"Take Me Out to the **Ball**game"
"Whene'er You Make a **Promise**"

Variation: Have the girls bring items for the other team to suggest. (You might get some very interesting contemporary song titles.)

Music Magic

How to play: Girls sit in a circle. One girl is "it" and leaves the room. The others decide on something in the room that "it" must touch. When "it" returns to the room, she walks around touching various objects, while the girls sing some prearranged song. As "it" gets "warm," the girls sing loudly; as she gets "cold," they sing softly. The girls try to guide "it" to the object by the degree of loudness or softness in their singing. When "it" correctly guesses the object, another girl is chosen to be "it."

Song Pictures

You need: A numbered paper plate or paper circle, a crayon or marker, and a piece of paper for each player.

How to play: Girls sit in circle formation. Each girl has a numbered paper plate or paper on which to draw a picture that illustrates a song title. Allow five minutes for drawing the picture. When the time limit is up, each girl passes her plate to the girl on her right, who writes the number of the plate and the name of the song on her slip of paper. Allow a few minutes for this. Plates are again passed to the right until all girls have had a chance to see every picture. The girl who has the largest number of correct song titles on her list wins.

Variation: Pictures are drawn and plates are passed to the right, but each player sings a line from the song represented instead of writing its title. If she cannot sing a line, the plate is again passed to the right. The game continues until all but one player has been eliminated.

Twenty Questions

How to play: One player leaves the room. The others decide on something that can be classified as animal, vegetable, or mineral. Suppose the group decides on a Girl Scout pin. The player must guess by asking questions that can be answered by yes or no. She is allowed twenty questions. Questions and answers might go like this: "Is it mineral?" "Yes." "Is there more than one?" "Yes." "Is it used only by Girl Scouts?" "Yes." And so on until she guesses the correct answer or has asked twenty questions.

Variation: Use objects that are visible to the group.

SITTING GAMES

 *Buzz*

How to play: Girls are seated in a circle. Count in numerical order around the circle. As a girl comes to a number which is a multiple of five or seven, such as five, seven, ten, fourteen, fifteen, or any number ending in seven, she must say "buzz" instead of that number. If she says "buzz" in the wrong place, or says a number where she should have said "buzz," she is out of the circle. A girl can reenter the game when the next girl is out, or the game can be played until the last player in the game wins.

Card Concentration

You need: A deck of cards.

How to play: Cards are placed face down randomly. Girls take turns turning over three cards, one at a time. The object is to turn up three cards in numerical order. Ace is low, or one. For example, a run could consist of ace, two, and three of any suit, or a six, seven, and eight of any suit. When a girl does not turn over a run, she turns the cards face down and the next girl takes her turn. It helps to remember location and value of cards as they are turned up. The winner is the girl with the most runs.

Dots and Triangles

You need: Paper and pencil for each pair of girls.

How to play: Draw a triangular grid of dots, with eight dots on each side. In turn, each girl draws a connecting line between two adjacent dots, the object being to construct a triangle. When a girl completes a triangle, she places her initials inside the triangle and is given another turn. When all the dots have been connected, the girl with the most triangles wins.

Magazine Message

You need: Magazines or newspapers, scissors, glue, and paper for each girl.

How to play: The game leader cuts single words, phrases, or pictures from a magazine or newspaper to prepare a question or message for girls to answer. Each girl prepares an answer by using words, pictures, and phrases from the magazine in a timed period. Rotate the role of questioner and share answers in the group.

This English game might be known in America as pass the beanbag or pass the ball, while in Canada it is pass the broom. In other countries it is known as pass the bone, pass the hot potato, pass the candle, or pass the fish.

You need: Something to represent the fox, such as a beanbag.

How to play: Girls sit in a circle, with a leader in the center. The "fox" is passed rapidly from girl to girl. At the clap of the hand, the fox is passed in the opposite direction. Girls must pass the fox as quickly and as smoothly as possible. Whoever drops or fumbles the object must either pay a forfeit (i.e., perform a stunt) or go to the center of the circle, depending on the way the group decides to play the game.

Variation: The girl in the center is blindfolded. Besides clapping to change direction, she can say "fox" and the girl holding the item at that moment is "it."

Rainmakers

You need: A game leader who knows the sequence of motions that is outlined for this game.

How to play: This activity is a good one for inclement weather, in the hope that if it "rains" inside, it will stop raining outside. It works well with large groups. The girls are seated. The game leader explains that everyone must follow her lead if they are to make a good rain. As she passes, they are to do the motions she is doing at the tempo she is doing them. The motions are:

Rubbing palms in a forward/backward motion
    slowly/softly
    louder/faster
Snapping fingers
    slowly/softly
    more loudly/swiftly
Slapping thighs
    slowly/softly
    more loudly/swiftly
    slowly/softly
Snapping fingers
    loudly/swiftly
    more softly/more slowly
Rubbing palms
    loudly/swiftly
    more softly/more slowly
Silence

Ring Game

You need: A rope or string long enough to go around the circle, with a ring on it.

How to play: The group sits in circle formation. One girl is "it" and stands in the center. Each girl has her hands on the rope. The ring is passed around the circle. The girls keep their hands moving to hide the position of the ring. "It" tries to guess the position of the ring. The girl who holds the ring when "it" locates it must be "it" the next time.

Variations: Hands may be placed behind the back and the string is outside the circle. The game can also be played without the string. The girls mime passing the ring to each other around the circle.

WORD GAMES

Giggling Gertie

You need: A handkerchief.

How to play: A circle is formed. One girl is selected to be in the center. She laughs and tosses a handkerchief into the air. The group starts laughing. All girls continue to laugh as long as the handkerchief is in the air. The instant it touches the floor, all faces must become expressionless. Anyone caught smiling is out. Play until one girl is left.

Finish the Song

How to play: The group is divided into two teams. Team A starts singing a song. When the game leader raises her hand, the singing stops. Team B must then take up the song at that point and finish it. If B cannot finish it, A starts the next song. But if Team B is successful, its members start the next song and Team A must complete it.

Mixed Messages

You need: Pencil and paper for each girl.

How to play: Have each girl write a question, beginning with the word "why." Collect the questions. Have each girl write an answer to her question that begins with the word "because." Collect the answers. Shuffle each stack of questions and answers and give each player one answer and one question. Have each girl read the question and the answer that she has aloud to the group.

Variation: After reading the mixed messages, have the girls match the questions and the answers.

Rainbow Colors

How to play: One girl sits in the middle of a circle of players. She calls out a color from the rainbow and points to a girl in the circle. The girl has until the count of seven to come up with the name of something that is that color (for example, red might bring a response of apple). The girl in the middle changes places with the girl who misses an object.

Smile

You need: A coin.

How to play: Girls are divided into two teams. Teams line up facing each other about ten feet apart. One team is named Heads, and the other is named Tails. The game leader tosses a coin and calls out the side that turns up. If it comes up heads, the Heads laugh and smile, while the Tails must keep a straight face. The Heads attempt to make the Tails laugh. All Tails who laugh must join the other team. The coin is tossed again. Allow approximately half a minute for each round.

Taboo

You need: A list of words and related subjects that the group decides upon prior to playing.

How to play: The object of this game is not to use the words that the group has decided are taboo. In partners or teams, talk about an assigned topic for a given period of time. It is more interesting if the subject has something to do with the taboo words. For example, the taboo words are "tent," "counselor," "food," "fun," and "Girl Scout," and the subject is camp. Each time a word is used that is taboo, the player or team is penalized one point. The lowest score wins.

Talking Stick

You need: A stick over two feet long or a yardstick.

How to play: The group sits in a circle. The stick is given to a girl to start, and she begins a story while moving her hands up the stick, hand over hand. When she reaches the top, she stops and passes the stick to the next girl, who continues the story. Continue around the circle until all have had a turn.

Vacation

How to play: Girls are seated in a circle. The game leader begins by saying, "I'm going on vacation, and I'm taking _____ (anything can be named)." The girl to her right then says, "I'm going on vacation, and I'm taking (*the first girl's item*) and _____ ." This continues around the circle, each girl naming the previous items given, plus her own. If a girl misses an item, she moves out of the circle and the game continues, or she can reposition herself for another try. The object is to go around the complete circle with no one forgetting an item, or to declare the girl who remembers the most items in the correct order the winner.

CHAPTER 4

ACTIVE GAMES FOR INDOORS AND OUTDOORS

CHALLENGE AND INITIATIVE GAMES

These are fun and challenging games that can pull a group together, build teamwork, and encourage an individual or group to try the untried. Some of these games may require someone to act as a spotter for safety.

 *Capture the Flag*

You need: A large area with some spots for hiding, two colored flags, and one girl to act as a judge and referee.

How to play: Divide the group into two teams of equal size, playing ability, and leadership ability. Each team should select a leader. Determine the playing boundaries, and mark a centerline across the playing area. Locate a jail for each side on the opposing team's territory an equal distance from the centerline, and have each team name a jailer.

Each team hides its flag on its side of the playing field. Flag guards can stand no closer than three feet to the team flag. The object is for a person from one side to cross the centerline and "capture" the other team's flag and return it to her own side without being caught. A girl from the opposite side may be "jailed" if caught outside her territory. The girl tagging must say "caught" three times. To get a teammate out of jail, a girl must run to the jail and tag her, saying "free." Since each team's jail is on the opposing team's territory, a player can be tagged and put into jail while rescuing a teammate.

 *Cover It*

You need: A clear plastic bowl filled with water, a dime, and pennies or chips for each team.

How to play: Place the dime in six to eight inches of water in the bowl. Each team has at least ten pennies. The first girl drops a penny into her team's bowl in an attempt to cover the dime. If she is not successful, the next girl tries. The team using the least amount of pennies to cover its dime can be declared the winner.

Lost at Sea

You need: A large field to run across; a circular piece of cardboard approximately three feet across (or a tire) for each group to use as a ship.

How to play: Divide into groups of no more than eight to ten girls. Each group is given a "ship," which all members must grasp onto. The group is to run with its "ship" until the game leader shouts, "Shark!" Then all jump on board the ship. The first group to get all their feet on board gets a point. Repeat this several times, with the first group reaching the finish line getting five points. Allow the group to strategize and try again.

Silent Steal

You need: A dark room or blindfolds and a soft object such as a ball or towel.

How to play: Divide the group into "protectors" and "stealers." The protectors must wear blindfolds or the game must take place in a dark room. Place the protectors around the object about three feet apart. The stealers are to sneak by the protectors to get the object. The protectors are to tag the stealers if they sense or hear them. This is a game of listening skills and cooperation, as the girls must be very quiet to be successful. If the stealers are too good, have the stealers add some things to the ground, such as leaves or wadded-up paper, for them to navigate.

Shoe Scramble

You need: A blindfold for each person.

How to play: Have all girls remove their shoes and place them in a corner. Blindfold each girl and mix up the pile of shoes. Have each girl find her own shoes in the pile.

Variation: Have girls work in pairs and find their partners' shoes and place them on their partners' feet while blindfolded.

Water Balloon Toss

You need: A balloon filled with water halfway and tied for each pair of girls, an outdoor space, and a warm day.

How to play: Have partners line up facing each other in two parallel lines. The game begins by having girls in one line toss balloons to their partners. As the balloon is caught, each partner must take one step back. The object is not to be the one to miss the balloon. The last team to have a water balloon in the air is the winner.

You need: Room for rotating the group at stations, a yard-long round stick, chalk, soft ground, and a handkerchief or paper.

How to play: Each challenge can be presented on its own, or as a part of a challenge course or wide game. These are great rainy-day activities. You might post directions at stations, or have someone explain the activity at each station. Or you can do them as a group. (Note the ones that call for a spotter.)

Ankle Sit:

The girl crosses her legs at the ankles. She folds her arms. She sits down and stands up.

Fishing Heron:

Have the girls do this challenge in a soft area. The girl places a handkerchief or paper (the fish) 12 inches above the ground. She holds her right ear with her left hand and holds her left foot behind her with her right hand. She touches the fish with her nose when bending over. (A spotter may be needed to keep the girl from landing on her beak!)

Hand to Hand:

Each girl stands at arm's length from her partner, face to face. Each girl's feet must be together. The object is to get the partner to lose her balance, using only the hands. Score this on a point basis (moving feet is a minus point, body contact is a minus point), or go for the best two out of three rounds.

Variation: Start with palms together, keeping contact at all times, and try to get the other girl off balance.

Heels in Glue:

The girl faces a wall. She stands with her feet together and toes six inches from the wall. She touches knees to the wall without raising her heels, which are "glued" to the floor. If successful, she tries for a greater distance.

Leg Balance:

The girl stands on one foot and extends the other foot and leg out behind the body while exending arms horizontally to the sides. She attains a position with the leg fully extended and the toes pointed; the upper body is horizontal to the ground. She holds this position for five to ten seconds, then tries the same thing with the other leg.

Pretzel:

Have the girl hold the ends of a two-foot stick in front of her body. She is to climb through the stick one leg at a time and, by moving the stick up over the back of her head, return to the start position. Have her try this move in reverse as well.

Squatting Jump:
The girl draws a chalk mark on the floor, or places a string on the ground. She stands about one foot behind the line with feet together. She bends her knees enough to grasp her ankles with both hands. She jumps over the line. The girl can reposition herself a greater distance from the line as an additional challenge.

Through the Loop:
With hands held together in front of the body, the girl steps through her arms one leg at a time and then back again while keeping her hands together.

Wring the Washrag:
Have two girls, approximately the same size, face each other with joined hands overhead. They turn, one going under her left arm and the other under her right arm. They should be back-to-back. With arms still raised, they continue to turn in the same direction until they face each other again.

JUMP ROPE GAMES

There are many jump rope games that can be played by a group. Make jump ropes a part of your troop equipment. The following games are popular with many ages:

 *Follow the Leader*

How to play: Jumpers stand in a line in front of the rope. Two players turn the rope. The leader jumps in with the turn and repeats a rhyme of her choice before jumping out. The next girl must jump in and repeat the rhyme while jumping and then exit. If a girl cannot "follow the leader" accurately, she takes the place of one of the rope turners.

 *Rock the Cradle*

How to play: The rope turners allow the rope to swing back and forth in a low arc, just brushing the ground. Each girl in turn must jump the rope two or three times and jump out without catching the rope in her feet. When everyone has had a turn, the rope height is raised a few inches and the round is repeated. The height of the rope is increased for each round. The girl completing all rounds successfully is the winner.

Time

How to play: The group forms a circle representing the face of a clock. A single rope turner stands in the middle of the circle holding one end of the rope. The rope is to be the second hand on the clock; it is rotated parallel to the ground in a large circle. Twelve girls, representing the numbers on the clock, try to jump over the rope while it is being rotated by the rope turner. Any girl who touches or stops the rope is out. If played with less than 13 girls, the group should decide which hours are to be represented on the clock face and station themselves accordingly. If there are more than 12 girls, one of the girls on the sidelines may rotate in. The last girl on the clock face is the winner.

Pass

How to play: Two girls turn the rope while the other girls take turns running in. In the first round, each girl runs in, jumps once, and exits. In the second round, each girl must jump the rope twice before exiting. Girls who miss are out and must become a rope turner. The girl who lasts the longest wins.

Chinese Jump Rope

See page 69 for instructions on how to make this type of jump rope and how to play the game.

Chinese Kick Rope

This is a favorite rope game played by young people in China.

How to play: Two girls hold the rope between them at waist height. The other girls take turns kicking at the rope, facing forward and then backward. If a girl can reach the rope with both kicks, the rope is raised a little higher on the next turn.

Girls who cannot kick the rope are eliminated, until only one girl remains.

MOVEMENT GAMES

 *Barnyard Bedlam*

You need: A paper bag for each group and a bag of peanuts in their shells or a lot of small pine or fir cones. Scatter the peanuts or cones in a designated area, such as a large meadow or playing field.

How to play: This is a great, noisy activity for large groups of people. Divide the group into teams. Each group represents an animal, and must practice making the noise of its animal. Each team must select a captain, who carries the team's paper bag. Explain the boundaries of the search. At a signal, the total group rushes out to the seeded area. If a peanut is discovered, a player must stand and point at it and make her team's animal noise. The team captain is the *only* one who can pick up peanuts. The bedlam continues until all the peanuts are found or a set time is up. Have each team count its peanuts; the team with the most peanuts is the winner. (See "Nature Awareness Games," pages 97–104, for an adaptation of this game.)

 *Bridges*

You need: Music that can be stopped and started (such as with a radio or tape deck) by a game leader.

How to play: Four girls make two bridges by extending arms and clasping hands. As the music plays, the other girls walk, run, or skip under the bridges. When the music stops, the bridges quickly lower their arms and try to catch a player. Any girls caught form new bridges. If a girl is caught and no partner is available to make a bridge with her, she stays out of the game until another player is caught to become a bridge with her. The last girl caught wins.

 *Daisy, Daisy . . . Juliette*

How to play: Girls form a single circle. One girl is selected to be "it" and stands outside the circle. Girls in the circle are in a squatting position facing inward. "It" walks around the outside of the circle saying "Daisy" as she taps each girl on the head. When she taps a girl and says "Juliette," she immediately starts to run clockwise around the circle. The girl who was tapped must run counter-clockwise. The object is for "it" or "Juliette" to reach the space vacated by "Juliette." The girl who reaches the space first stays there, while the other girl becomes or remains "it." A girl can only be "it" three times in a row.

Eskimo Bank—A Game for the Snow

You need: Nuts, cones, or large buttons.

How to play: A large circular hole is dug in the snow. An equal number of objects are given to each girl. One girl, the "banker," stands near the hole or "bank." The other girls stand about ten feet from the hole, and each takes her turn at trying to pitch all her objects into the bank. Each girl receives from the banker as many objects as she succeeds in pitching into the bank. The game continues. As girls run out of objects, they are eliminated. The girl left with the largest number of objects becomes the banker and opens her own bank.

Magic Ball—A Scottish Game

You need: A ball and stones for boundaries.

How to play: A "river" ten feet wide is marked out with stones. (A driveway or playground markers could be used instead of stones.) The girls are divided into two teams, or more than two if the group is large. All teams are on one side of the river. The game leader puts the ball in play by throwing it high in the air. Whoever catches it before it touches the ground shares its magic properties and is able to walk across the river. From the other side she throws the ball back across the river to one of her own teammates while members of the other teams try to intervene. If no one catches the ball before it touches the ground, the game leader puts it in play again. Anyone stepping into the river in the excitement of the game "gets dunked"; if she is dunked three times, she is considered "all wet" and must drop out. The team that first gets all its members safely across the river wins.

Musical Laps

You need: Sit-upons and a tape deck or radio or musical instrument.

How to play: Place sit-upons on the floor in a row (one less than the number of girls). Girls walk around the sit-upons while the music is playing. When the music stops, girls scramble for a seat on the sit-upons. Each time the music starts, one sit-upon should be removed. The number of girls remains the same. The game leader should watch to see that girls do not get too enthusiastic!

 *The Ocean Is Stormy—A Danish Game*

You need: String or chalk to mark circles.

How to play: The girls form pairs. Every pair except one stands within its own small circle, which is marked on the floor or on the ground. Each pair, with the exception of the odd pair, chooses the name of a fish. The odd pair are the "whales" and walk about the room, calling the names of fishes. When a pair's name is called, these girls leave their circle and walk behind the whales. After all names have been called or after the whales have called all the names they can think of, they cry, "The ocean is stormy!" The whales and all fish walking behind them rush to find a circle. The two girls left without a circle become the whales for the next game.

Variation: When the whales cry, "The ocean is stormy!" all fish must find a circle but no fish can return to the same partner or the same circle.

 *Pyramid Soccer*

You need: Three to five plastic bottles and one soccer or kick ball.

How to play: Arrange the bottles to form a pyramid in the middle of a circle. One girl is designated "goalie" and must defend the pyramid. The girls forming the circle kick the ball toward the center and try to knock the pyramid down. The girl who knocks the pyramid down becomes the new "goalie."

 *Sardines*

How to play: The group is divided into partners, and one pair are chosen to be the "hiders." The "hiders" are given two minutes in which to hide. Then the other partners start out to find them. The partners must stay together. When partners find the "hiders," they join them in their hiding place. This continues until all partners have found the "hiders." The first partners to find the "hiders" become the "hiders" for the next game.

Spot the Lion—An African Game

You need: A small piece of masking tape or adhesive tape.

How to play: Teams of five to eight players are formed. Each team is given its own corner or place. On signal, the players scatter and stand with their eyes shut. The game leader runs around tapping each girl lightly on the back; at the same time she puts a piece of tape on one of the girls who, unknown to herself, becomes the "lion."

When everyone has been tapped, the game leader shouts, "The lion is loose!" All girls then open their eyes and run around trying to spot the lion. When a girl does so, she hurries to her team corner, trying not to arouse the lion's suspicion. If a girl suspects that she is the lion (no girl is allowed to touch her own back to find out whether or not she is the lion), she goes to the center of the room and roars loudly. When this happens, all players must freeze. If the girl who roared is the lion, the game is over. If the girl who roared is not the lion, the game continues for one minute before time is called. The winning team is the one with the most girls in its corner when the game ends.

Variation: Continue playing until only the lion is left.

 Sticky Popcorn[2]

How to play: The game leader tells the girls that they are popcorn kernels. They start out by "popping" or jumping about slowly, and as the heat is increased (the game leader can call out "hotter"), they hop faster. This is a special "sticky" popcorn. When girls bump into each other, they stick together and continue to hop. They can continue to grow into a giant popcorn ball.

NIGHT GAMES OR IN-THE-DARK GAMES

 *Flashlight Tag*

You need: Flashlights for each "hider" and each team of "seekers."

How to play: Play in an area with well-defined boundaries. "Hiders" are given a head start to elude "seekers." They must flash their lights once every minute. (They have the option of changing hiding places.) Teams of "seekers" go in search of "hiders" and tag them when they find them. Teams must stay together in the dark. Captured "hiders" can run and hide after being tagged. The winning team is the one with the most number of tags for the game. This is a game for older girls and should be played in an area with safe terrain.

---

[2]From *The Cooperative Sports and Games Book,* by Terry Orlick. Copyright 1978 by Terry Orlick. Reprinted by permission of Pantheon Books, a division of Random House, Inc.

Night "O" Letter Scramble

You need: A site that has been walked for safety hazards, paper and a pencil for each team, a set of orienteering clues, orienteering stations, an orienteering map, a flashlight for each team, and orienteering markers for each station. (These could be marked with reflector tape.) At each orienteering station, there should be a letter clue. The letters all together should spell a word.

How to play: This is a game for accomplished orienteerers. Divide girls into teams of three, with experience and leadership abilities evenly distributed. At the starting point, give girls the list of clues and locations of the stations and let them plot their route on the map. Explain that there will be a letter at each station. When they have visited the stations they should be able to unscramble the word.

Variation: Give word clues and the girls can unscramble the sentence, or give animal names and the group can create a food chain.

Night Map and Compass

You need: Paper and pens for each team. At each station, have a map, flashlight, and bearings to the next station. A site that has designated boundaries and no hazards. Adults or girls can be stationed to help define the boundaries and ensure safety.

How to play: This is a map and compass game, not a formal orienteering game. Each group starts off at a different station. They read the clues, take the degree readings, and determine the paces needed to advance to the next station. At each station they pick up a clue, as in the night "O" letter scramble. In introducing the game, point out how the constellations have been used to guide sailors and travelers throughout history. Challenge the girls to use the stars as reference points in their night game.

How to play: Divide the group into teams. The total group stands in a circle facing outward, with a leader standing in the center of the circle. Girls advance about 50 yards and stop. On signal, they start to creep back toward the leader. They try to get as close as possible to the leader without being seen. The leader may turn around but may not move from the center. If the leader sees a girl moving, that girl must return to her original starting point and begin again. When a girl is motionless, she is "invisible." On signal, the girls must stand up wherever they are. The girls nearest the leader score points for their teams.

Variation: Advancing statues. Two parallel lines are marked out about 20 feet apart. Girls stand in back of one line; a leader stands on the other, her back to the group. From time to time the leader turns around to look at the girls. When the leader is not looking, each girl advances toward the leader's line. When the leader is looking, girls stand like statues. On noticing the slightest movement by a statue, the leader tells that statue to go back to the starting line. The first girl to reach the leader's line wins.

TAG GAMES

 *Back-to-Back Tag*

How to play: A girl is chosen to be "it" and can tag anyone not standing back-to-back with another girl. No one may stand by the same person longer than five seconds. When a girl is tagged, she becomes "it."

 *Blob Tag*[3]

You need: A large playing area with defined boundaries.

How to play: The girl who is "it" starts the game by tagging another girl and grabbing her hand after the tag. Together, the growing blob works to bring other girls into its chain. The blob can strategize how to capture girls, and even divide into smaller parts in order to capture its prey.

---

[3]Excerpt from the *New Games Book,* by Andrew Fluegelman, copyright 1976 by the Headlands Press, Inc. Used by permission of Doubleday, a division of Bantam, Doubleday, Dell Publishing Group, Inc.

 *Color Tag*

How to play: All girls stand in an open area. The game leader begins by asking them to touch or point to something that is a specific color, such as green. Everyone should quickly touch, stand close to, or point to something with that color. Girls who are unable to do so are out. The game leader continues to call out colors until one girl remains.

 *Hug Tag*[4]

You need: Space for a tag game.

How to play: Play a game of tag, with one girl designated "it." Girls are safe only when they are hugging another girl. This game works best with younger girls and older mixed groups!

Variation: Change the number of bodies required for a safe hug.

 *"It" Tag*

You need: Defined boundaries, indoors or outdoors.

How to play: Every player is "it." If one girl tags another girl, the tagged girl must take a seat. If two girls tag each other at the same time, both girls must sit down. Girls who are seated can still participate by tagging girls who come near them. The last girl to be tagged wins.

Snake in the Grass[5]

You need: A grassy field or a clean floor space.

How to play: Define the boundaries for the snake area. The snake lies on her stomach with everyone gathered around touching her on some part of her body. The game leader shouts, "Snake in the grass!" and everyone runs to avoid being tagged. When the slithering snake tags someone, she becomes a snake, too. Girls must keep within the boundaries. Snakes can hiss to add excitement. The last girl tagged becomes the snake in the grass for the next game. Caution girls to avoid stepping on the snake's fingers as they dash about.

[4,5]Excerpt from the *New Games Book,* by Andrew Fluegelman, copyright 1976 by the Headlands Press, Inc. Used by permission of Doubleday, a division of Bantam, Doubleday, Dell Publishing Group, Inc.

You need: Handkerchief or beanbag.

How to play: Girls are divided into two teams. Teams line up facing each other about 20 to 30 feet apart. Girls in each line are numbered so that there is a girl numbered 1, 2, 3, etc., on each team. In the center, halfway between the two lines, a handkerchief or beanbag is placed. The leader calls a number and the girls with that number rush to the center. The first one to reach the handkerchief grabs it and runs back to her line. She is safe anywhere in the line. The other girl tries to tag her before she can get back.

Scoring: If the player with the handkerchief is tagged, one point is scored for the opposing side. If the girl with the handkerchief gets back to her line safely, two points are scored for her team. The team with the highest score wins.

Variation: Instead of a handkerchief, use two to ten objects (acorns, maple seeds, sassafras leaves, etc.) or pictures. The leader calls the name of the object or picture. Then she calls a number. Girls with that number run to the center and try to snatch the object named. No tagging. Score two points for the team whose player brings back the correct object; score one point for the opposing team if the wrong object is snatched and brought back.

RELAY GAMES

CHAPTER **5**

WHAT IS A RELAY?

Many games are played as relays. A relay is a series of individual efforts that accumulate in credit for the team. They are a great way to build team spirit and emphasize the importance of individual contributions to team effort.

Relays can be adapted for a group of any size and to almost any meeting place, indoors or outdoors. Some relays are played on a predetermined course, while others just need a starting and finish line. Many use objects, such as a beanbag or ball, which are passed from hand to hand (or foot to foot), while others involve performing certain actions or demonstrating special skills or knowledge.

Although most relays involve running, there are many variations of movement possible, depending upon the age level, skill, and enthusiasm of the players. Walking back-to-back, moving like animals, hopping, and crawling are some variations. Relays also lend themselves to controlled water games, as long as you match swimming skill levels with the type of relay.

Generally, a relay game has a clearly marked starting and turn-around line. Because of the competitive nature of the game, it is best to have a designated referee. Often there will be unequal teams, and each girl should clearly understand if she must run more than once to even up the play. To assist in determining a winner, the referee can request that a team be seated or raise hands as soon as all girls have completed the game.

FORMS OF RELAYS

There are five commonly used relay forms: the file, the circle, the zigzag, the partner, and the shuttle. Each basic relay form is described prior to introducing a selection of relay games.

File Form Relay

Girls on each team line up, one behind the other, perpendicular to the starting line. Girl No. 1 goes forward to the designated turning point and returns to her team, tagging girl No. 2. This continues until all girls on a team have had a turn. The team finishing first is the winner.

Circle Relay Form

Girls on each team stand or sit in their own circle. They are numbered off clockwise. In a running relay, No. 1 jumps up and runs clockwise around the outside of the circle. When she returns to her place, she tags No. 2, and sits down. Girl No. 2 jumps up and runs around the circle, and so forth, until the girls have gone around the circle. This relay may also be played by passing an object around the circle until it returns to girl No. 1. The team finishing first is the winner.

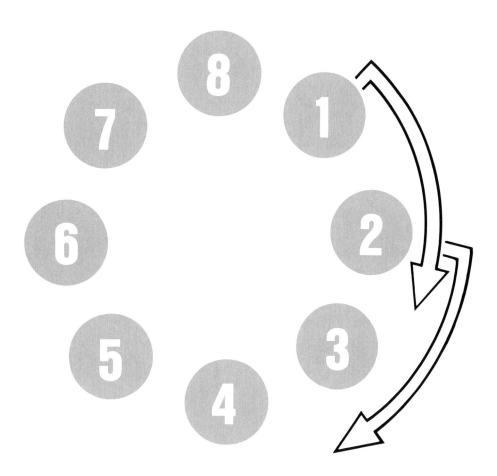

Zigzag Relay Form

Each team forms two lines that face the center. Number off as follows: No. 1 on one side, No. 2 on the other, No. 3 back on the first side, and so forth. Girls should stand so that each is opposite an empty spot in the line across from her (see the illustration). On a signal, an object is passed as follows: No. 1 to No. 2 to No. 3 to No. 4 and so on, zigzagging down the line. The game can end when the object reaches the last girl on the team, or when the object returns to the starting player.

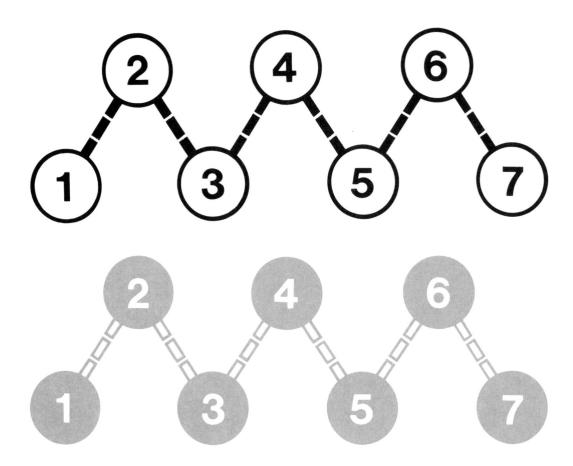

Partner Relay Form

Each girl chooses a partner. Teams consist of an equal number of sets of partners, standing side-by-side in file formation. The game leader indicates the method of travel, such as running, skipping, hopping, or jumping with feet together. The first set of partners from each team move together, hands joined, upon signal. They travel to a designated spot and return to the starting line to tag the next set of partners. This continues until all of the partners have the opportunity to participate. The winning team is the one to move through the partner sets first.

Each team counts off by two's. Each team forms two file lines that face each other, with the even numbers facing the odd numbers. The distance between lines can vary according to the type of shuttle relay. On a signal, No. 1 runs and hands an object to No. 2 on her team, then takes her place at the end of the even numbers line. No. 2 runs and hands the object to No. 3 on her team and goes to the end of the odd numbers line. This continues until all girls are back in their original places.

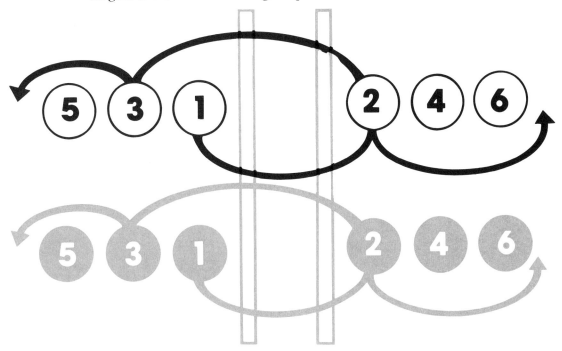

RELAY GAMES

 *Beanbag Relay*

Relay form: File.

You need: Beanbags. (See page 68.)

How to play: In file formation, each girl tries to walk, skip, hop on one foot, or run from the starting line to a turn-around point and return to the next in line while balancing a beanbag on her head with her hands behind her back. If the beanbag falls off, the girl must pick it up and place it back on her head before moving on. The game continues until all girls on a team have had a turn.

Variations: Balance the beanbag on a shoulder or between the elbows while moving. The type of movement can be determined by the referee, so that each team member has a different way to travel with the beanbag.

Bottle Filler Relay

Relay form: File.

You need: Five plastic bottles, a bucket of water, a funnel, and a plastic or metal cup for each team. A judge at the turn-around line.

How to play: Set up stations with five plastic bottles and a funnel for each team at the turn-around line. At the starting line, each team should have a large bucket of water and a cup. On signal, player No. 1 on each team fills the cup with water, and runs to the team's bottle station. She empties her cup in a bottle, using a funnel, and then returns to tag and hand off the cup to the No. 2 player. She fills it and runs to the team's bottles. The first team to fill all five bottles wins. This is a game best played outdoors.

Clean Sweep Relay

Relay form: File.

You need: A broom and a minimum of two inflated balloons for each team.

How to play: Teams line up with a broom and a balloon. The No. 1 player proceeds to move the balloon with the broom to the turn-around line and back. If she touches the other balloon, she must return to the starting line. In the event a balloon breaks, she must return to the starting line as well. When the first player crosses the starting line with her balloon, she hands off the broom to player No. 2.

Cotton Ball Relay

Relay form: Zigzag.

You need: One spoon for each team member and a bag of cotton balls for each team. A clock to time the play.

How to play: Each team should line up in a close zigzag formation. Each team member is given a spoon. The team member on one end picks up a cotton ball and places it on her spoon. It is then passed down the line in a zigzag pattern (see the illustration on page 52) from spoon to spoon. If the cotton ball is dropped at any time during the passing, the team must begin again. The team to get the most cotton balls to the end, in a timed period, wins.

Crazy Groceries

Relay form: Circle.

You need: Paper and pencil for each team. A game leader.

How to play: Each team is seated in a circle. Each girl writes down the name of something sold in a grocery store, but mixes up the letters in the word. On a signal, each girl passes her slip to the girl on her right, who tries to decipher the word correctly. The game leader signals after one minute and the slips are passed to the right again, whether they have been deciphered or not. Words that have been correctly deciphered can be placed in the middle of the circle, until all words are deciphered. Points are scored for the team whose members decipher all their slips first.

Variation: Other topics can be used for determining the words, such as the contents of a first-aid kit or equipment for a hike.

Crossing the Ice

Relay form: File.

You need: Two sheets of newspaper for each team, each sheet folded to a size a little larger than a player's foot.

How to play: The folded papers represent cakes of ice. On signal, the No. 1 player of each team places one piece of paper on the floor, steps on it, and places the other piece on the floor for the other foot. She then retrieves the first piece of paper, pushes it forward, and steps on it. This continues until she has reached the turn-around line and returns to her team to tag and hand off the papers to the No. 2 player.

If a girl steps on the floor instead of the paper, she falls into the water, and must return to the starting line to try again. Younger girls may put both feet on the same paper; older girls cannot place both feet on the same paper at any time. The first team to finish wins.

Dress Up Relay

Relay form: File.

You need: A large assortment of loose clothing, enough for one outfit per team member.

How to play: Place assorted clothing into a large pile. On signal, No. 1 players race to the pile and "get dressed." All clothing put on must be properly tied, buttoned, and zipped. Player No. 1 returns to her team and tags player No. 2, who continues. The first team to become fully dressed wins.

Furnish That Room!

Relay form: Circle.

You need: Catalogs or magazines, scissors, glue, and a large piece of paper for each team.

How to play: Teams are seated in a circle, with the materials in the middle. Each team decides what kind of room it wants to furnish. On signal, each No. 1 player goes to the center of her circle and finds an item to furnish the team's room. She cuts it out and glues it on the paper. The No. 2 player then finds a different item to furnish the room. Play continues until every girl has had a turn. Additional rounds can be played by choosing different rooms to furnish.

Rooms are judged after each round on the basis of design, function, and suitability. A panel of judges awards up to five points for each category. The team having the best room may score up to fifteen points. When the game is over, total each team's scores. The team with the higher score wins.

Marble Relay

Relay form: Circle.

You need: A chair for each team member, 20 marbles per team in a cup, an additional cup for the circle.

How to play: Each team is seated in a circle. A cup containing twenty marbles is placed in the middle of each team. On signal, one member of each team designated "leader" removes a marble from the cup and places it in her cupped hand. She proceeds to pass it to the girl seated next to her. Each girl has to use a cupped hand to receive and pass the marble. When it reaches the last girl, she places the marble in an empty cup located near her seat. She then runs to the cup in the middle of the circle, removes another marble, and places it in the cupped hand of the leader. The passing begins again. The first team to place all the marbles in the empty cup wins. If a marble is dropped, it goes back to the leader.

 *Math Relay*

Relay form: File.

You need: One piece of chalk per team and a chalkboard. A referee with a calculator.

How to play: In teams, No. 1 players run to the chalkboard, write a two-digit number, and return to their team. Player No. 2 runs up to the board and writes another two-digit number directly under player No. 1's. This continues with each girl writing a different two-digit number under that of her team members. The last player on each team must add the numbers. Any team that correctly answers its math problem receives three points. The first team to reach 15 points or any other agreed-upon number divisible by three wins. If the answer is incorrect, the team gains no points and must still solve the problem.

Variation: Using letters of the alphabet in order, the first player runs to the board and writes a word beginning with the letter "a." She runs back and tags the second player, who comes to the board and writes a word beginning with the letter "b." Play continues until all 26 letters of the alphabet are used to write words. One point is given for each acceptable word.

 *Moving Cup Relay*

Relay form: File.

You need: A 12-foot length of string and a paper cup with a hole in the bottom for each team. Place the paper cup on the string and tie between two chairs as illustrated.

How to play: Each team lines up behind one of the chairs, with the paper cup at that end of the string. The No. 1 player must blow the cup from one end of the string to the other chair and back, before tagging player No. 2. The first team to finish wins.

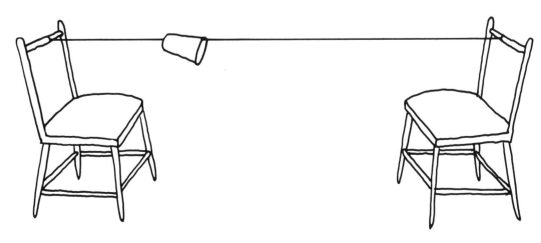

 *Partner Relay*

Relay form: Partner.

You need: A game leader with a whistle.

How to play: Divide into teams. Each team member selects a partner. On signal, with inner elbows hooked together, the first pair on each team begins walking quickly toward the turn-around line. When the game leader blows the whistle, the pair must stop and make a complete turn before resuming forward progress. The game leader can blow the whistle as often as she likes. The pair returns to the starting line in the same manner and tags the next pair in line. The first team to finish wins.

Variation: Have girls complete the relay in groups of three, with one member walking backward.

 *Relay Ball Game*

Relay form: File.

You need: One ball for each team.

How to play: Each team stands in file formation with a team leader sitting opposite about twenty feet away. She has the ball in her lap. On signal, the first player in line runs to her leader, picks up the ball, and returns to her place in the file line. She then throws the ball to the leader and goes to the end of the file line and sits down. When the ball returns to the leader's lap, the next player runs. The first team to finish a rotation wins.

 *Shoe Relay*

Relay form: File.

You need: Shoes from each girl.

How to play: Each girl removes her left shoe and places it in a pile at the turn-around point. (All shoes must be untied or unbuckled.) Teams line up at the starting line in file formation. On signal, the No. 1 player of each team runs to the shoe pile and finds her shoe. She then puts the shoe on and ties it. After she is finished, she returns to her team and tags the next player, who continues the relay. The first team to finish wins.

Variation: Instead of locating her own shoe and putting it on, have each girl find the shoe of the girl behind her in line and return to the starting line to place it on the teammate's foot.

Tennis Ball Pass

Relay form: File.

You need: A tennis ball for each team.

How to play: Teams stand in file formation. A tennis ball is passed from chin to chin, using no hands, from one end of the line to the other end. If the ball is dropped, it must be returned to the start of the line. The first team to pass the ball forward and backward wins.

Waddle Relay

Relay form: File.

You need: A small-to-medium-size ball for each team. (The balls should be the same size.)

How to play: Divide into teams. On signal, No. 1 players race against each other while carrying a ball between their knees. They must successfully reach the turn-around line, bounce the ball once, and return to their team with the ball once again between their knees and tag player No. 2. Player No. 2 continues. If the ball is dropped at any time, the player must go back and start over. The first team to have all players "waddle" the ball wins.

Which Fork?

Relay form: File.

You need: A spoon, fork, knife, soup spoon, salad fork, dessert fork, and knife for each team. A set of pictures of prepared foods that require different eating utensils. (An etiquette book might be needed to solve any disputes.)

How to play: Place the cutlery and pictures for each team's station on a table. Each team lines up file formation in line with their station. On signal, the No. 1 player from each team runs to the station, selects a picture of a prepared food, and places the appropriate piece, or pieces, of silverware on the picture. She returns to her team and tags the No. 2 player, and so forth. One point is given for each correct selection. The team that finishes first receives an additional point. The higher score wins.

Zigzag Ball Relay

Relay form: Zigzag.

You need: One rubber or tennis ball for each team.

How to play: Each team lines up in a double line, zigzag formation, facing each other. The No. 1 player on each team has a ball. On signal, she tosses the ball diagonally across to player No. 2, who tosses it across to player No. 3, and so on, to the end of the line. When the last girl catches the ball, she reverses the direction of travel. The team that gets the ball to the No. 1 player first receives one point. If the ball is dropped, it is returned to the start of the line. Play until a team reaches five points to determine the winner.

CHAPTER 6

TO AND FRO
AND IN-BETWEEN

WHY PLAY GAMES WHILE YOU TRAVEL AND WAIT?

Everyone has had the experience of waiting at an airport or bus station. Perhaps a group is passing time standing in line for a show, or waiting for a storm to pass, or is stranded somewhere unexpectedly. This kind of a delay on a group outing can become boring very fast. A good game leader always has something up her sleeve for these times.

Traveling from one place to another is often difficult for girls, whether it is a long bus ride to camp, a field trip to another state, or a plane ride to another city. Often the new experiences and geography can be capitalized upon in creating a game. Many of the games in this chapter can be played by one player or played while en route. However, keep in mind that frequent rest stops and leg stretches are also important.

EQUIPMENT FOR TRAVEL AND WAITING GAMES

A leader might consider keeping a special games pack for travel and waiting that can fit into a car glove box, a purse, or lunch box. It might include several pencils, pads of paper, a calculator, eraser, ruler, guidebook, maps of the area, and a compass. You might also carry magazines and newspapers. There are many games in this book, particularly in Chapter Three, that can be used for travel games. Enjoy yourselves.

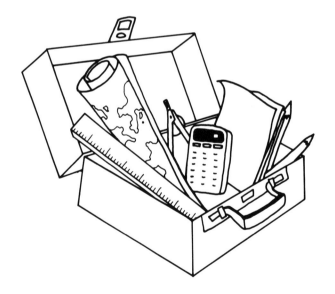

SAFETY FOR TRAVEL AND WAITING GAMES

Remember that when traveling in a bus or car, it is very dangerous for drivers to take their eyes off the road and their attention off the driving. For that reason, a driver should not participate in travel games, unless the vehicle is stopped. Passengers should also monitor their enthusiasm and actions so that they do not distract the driver. Do not play games that involve a lot of physical movement or airborne objects in moving vehicles.

The following are some other safety suggestions:

· Groups should also monitor their behavior in public waiting areas. Do not play games that infringe on other people's space or that disrupt places of business.
· Always have members of the group observe the buddy rule if individuals are leaving the group for any reason in a public space.
· Do not wear name tags in public places.
· Refer to *Safety-Wise* when planning any kind of travel or event with the troop or group.

TRAVEL AND WAITING GAMES

Billboards

You need: Paper and a pencil.

How to play: While traveling, pick words from billboards or business signs and create a sentence or story. This can be done individually, or with everyone in the group participating in turn.

Bingo Trail

You need: Index cards, pencils, ruler.

How to play: Have each girl draw a grid of twenty squares on a blank card. Each girl draws or writes an animal's name in a center square. Each girl has a different animal. She should place a check in a blank square each time her animal is seen, whether in a magazine illustration, on a billboard, or in print. The first girl to fill every square wins.

Variation: Use letters of the alphabet, cars, trees, or other things in place of animals.

 *Cars*

You need: Paper and pencil.

How to play: Have each girl select a brand or color of car or truck. Have them count the number of such vehicles they see on the road while traveling.

 *Clue*

How to play: The game leader spots something along the roadside. She gives others a clue about the object, such as size or color. Someone must guess the answer before the next mile marker.

 *Finish the Picture*

You need: Paper and pencils.

How to play: The first player draws a part of something she sees. She folds the paper to cover up her drawing and passes it to the next girl. After drawing part of something that she sees, this girl then folds the paper and passes it on to the next player. After everyone has had a turn, open up the paper and view the finished picture.

 *Hinkey Pinkey, or Hink Pink*

How to play: This game can be played anywhere, and is a great way to make the time pass, whether hiking up a steep hill or waiting in line. To play hink pink, which is the easiest form of the game, have someone give clues for two one-syllable words that rhyme. The clues do not need to rhyme. For example, the clue could be "swimmer's platter." The hink pink for this would be "fish dish." Two other examples are "evening beacon" for "night light" or "mollusk pathway" for "snail trail." The person who guesses the hink pink can make up the next one.

To play hinkey pinkey, give clues for two-syllable words that rhyme. For example, "lawful bird" would be "legal eagle," or "blooming strength" would be "flower power."

 *Letter License*

You need: Paper and pencils.

How to play: Have girls look at license plates with letters. Girls write down the first fifteen letters seen and make as many words as possible using those letters. Each letter can only be used once in a word.

Mapmaking

You need: Pads of paper, pencils, and a bumpy road.

How to play: Each girl places a pad of paper on her knees and holds the pencil on top of the paper. While traveling the bumpy road, the pencil will touch the paper and create lines that resemble a map. The girls complete the pencil markings by coloring or shading in the map when the vehicle stops. A contest can be held for the most original map.

Memories

You need: Magazines, pencils, and paper.

How to play: Girls look at a picture in a magazine for 25 seconds and then close it. Each girl lists the items she remembers in a two-minute time period. One point is given for each correct item, while two points are lost for each incorrect item. In a solo game, the girl can record her score and try to better it in the next round.

Numbers

How to play: While riding, girls look for numbers and keep a running total until the sum of one hundred is reached. Each girl looks out a different window of the vehicle to see who can reach one hundred first.

Odd License

You need: Paper and pencil.

How to play: Divide girls into two teams. One team is odd, the other even. In a timed period, teams receive one point for each odd-numbered or even-numbered license plate they spot. Out-of-state plates can count for two points.

Pairs

You need: Paper and pencil.

How to play: Have girls watch for pairs of things during a trip. For example, two mailboxes, two of the same billboard advertisements, two cows. The first girl to spot ten pairs wins.

 *Silly Places*

You need: A road map.

How to play: Have girls make up a silly story using geographical names from the map. The story must include at least ten places.

 *Things to Do with Maps*

You need: A map for each girl (if possible), markers, paper, and pencils.

How to play: Using a map, girls find names of places that have a color in their name, such as the Green River.

Variations: 1. Girls look for places that have animals or plants in their names.
 2. Have a girl make a list of nine cities on a map. Girls try to find each city within a given amount of time.
 3. Girls choose two cities far apart on a map. Using a marker, girls draw as many different routes between them as they can. Have them determine which is the shortest route and the longest route.

 *Zoo*

You need: Paper and pencils.

How to play: Girls write down a list of animals to be placed in a special "zoo." Each animal can be represented by an object. For example, an elephant is represented by a tree, a tiger by a gas pump, an ostrich by a police car. Types of objects cannot be used more than once to represent an animal.
 Using the prepared list, players can "capture" an "animal" by calling out its name. "I see an elephant" would be called out by a girl who spots a tree. The animal escapes if it is called by the wrong name, but it can be captured by another girl.

CHAPTER 7

SIMPLE GAMES TO MAKE AND PLAY

ASSORTED GAMES

 *Beanbags*

You need: Two pieces of material, approximately five inches square, dried beans, needle and thread, scissors.

How to make: Girls lay the two pieces of material together, right sides facing each other. They sew three of the sides together, leaving the fourth side open, and then turn the bag right-side out. Girls fill the bag two-thirds full with beans. They turn the raw edges inward on the fourth side and whipstitch the side together, as shown. (It is wise to reinforce the seams by double stitching if sewing by hand.)

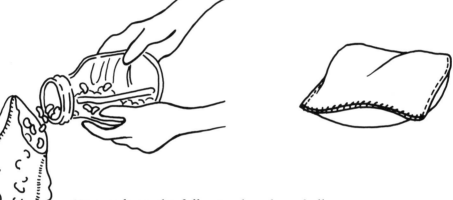

Have girls try the following beanbag challenges:

- Each girl throws the beanbag into the air and catches it after clapping hands twice.
- Each girl balances a beanbag on her head, a shoulder, or between the knees, and walks or hops from one point to another.
- Mark off two parallel lines at least fifty feet apart. Each girl stands facing a partner about five feet apart in the middle of the two lines. On signal, one partner tosses the beanbag to her partner. If the beanbag is caught, each takes a full step backward. The first pair to cross the parallel lines while moving backward wins.
- Girls form a circle. Place one magazine or sheet of newspaper for each girl, minus one, on the floor inside the circle. Place a beanbag on each magazine. On the leader's signal, girls move clockwise around the circle. The leader, who is blindfolded, stands on the outside of the circle and shouts "beanbag" or blows a whistle. At this point, each girl attempts to pick up a beanbag. The girl without one is out of the game. Remove one beanbag and one magazine from the playing area before resuming the game. The winner is the girl with the last beanbag.

You need: A twelve- to fifteen-foot length of ¼- to ½-inch elastic.

How to make: Sew or knot the elastic together to form a circle. This is a Chinese jump rope.

How to play: Two jump rope anchors stand in the middle of the rope circle and move away from each other, so that the rope is stretched taut between them at about eight inches off the ground. Girls line up to perform an agreed-upon sequence of jumps in and out of the oval formed by the Chinese jump rope as the anchors hold it. Such a sequence might involve:

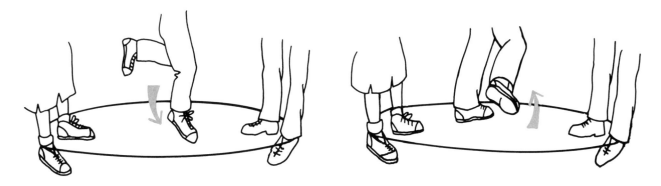

· Jumping into the oval on one foot, hopping out, and repeating the move on the other foot.

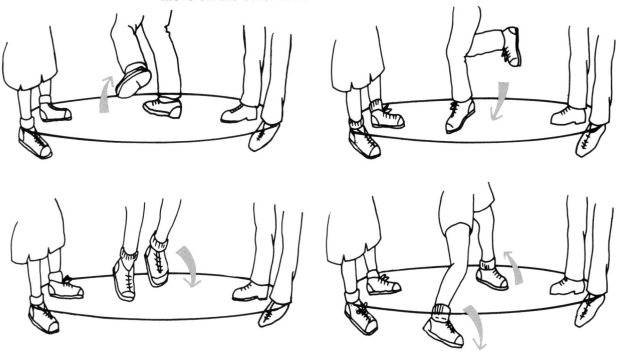

· Jumping into the oval using both feet, then jumping out, from both sides of the rope.

Jumping into the oval with both feet, spreading legs after leaping up so that feet land just outside the rope on either side, and jumping back into the ring with both feet again.

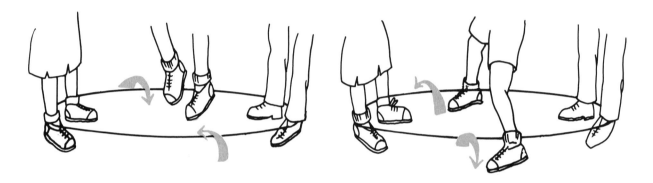

Girls' feet or legs should not make contact with the jump rope. If a girl touches the rope, she loses her place in line and must go to the end. The first girl to progress through the various jumps accurately wins. The game can be increased in difficulty by raising the height of the rope after successful completion of a round of jumps.

You need: A smooth patch of earth, a sidewalk, or a large piece of paper; a stick, a piece of chalk, or a pencil; 12 counters, such as beans or pebbles, for each person.

How to make: Construct a grid of five by six circles. Scratch it on the ground or in sand, mark it in chalk on cement, or draw it on paper.

How to play: Each girl places her 12 pieces in the circles on the playing grid. Initially, each girl cannot have more than two playing pieces in adjacent circles. Girls take turns moving their playing pieces one space at a time. This can be done in any direction, including diagonally. Unlike in checkers, jumping is not allowed. The goal is to place three pieces in a vertical or horizontal row, as shown. When this is accomplished, a girl may remove one of her opponent's pieces. The game is over when one girl is no longer able to line up three playing pieces, or when all of a girl's game pieces have been removed.

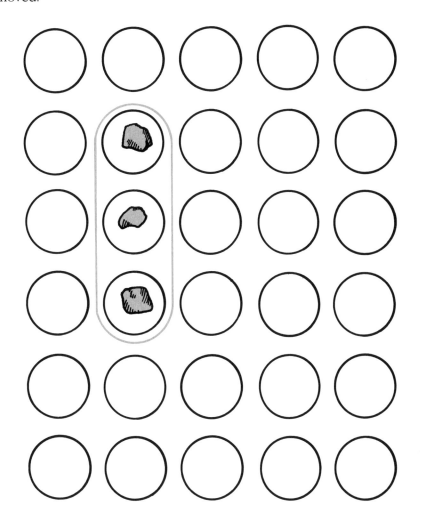

Egg Flat and Ball Game

You need: An egg carton or egg flat, a Ping-Pong ball, scissors, and markers.

How to make: Cut the lid off the egg carton or cut the egg flat down to nine to twelve compartments. Number each compartment consecutively.

How to play: Each girl holds the egg carton in front of her body. She places the Ping-Pong ball in the #1 compartment. She must toss the ball in the air, attempting to catch it in the #2 compartment. Count the number of attempts that it takes to move the ball through the nine compartments.

Variation: With two players, have the girls face each other about three feet apart. Each must toss the ball to her partner five times. Each time it lands in a compartment, the number is noted. Add up the numbers. The girl with the higher score wins.

Flying Frisbee

You need: A piece of heavy cardboard approximately a foot square; a drawing compass; scissors; crayons or paint.

To make: Inscribe a circle, 12 inches in diameter, on the heavy cardboard. Cut it out. Decorate it with paint or crayons.

To play: The following are challenges that can be played with a flying Frisbee:

1. Girls divide into teams. A player from each team gives the Frisbee a spin high into the air. The teams' Frisbee that goes the highest or farthest gets a point. The most points wins.

2. Girls divide into teams of five to eight players. The starting team is given the Frisbee. One member of the team throws the Frisbee high into the air. Members of the opposing team try to catch it. If the Frisbee is caught, one point is scored for that team. The Frisbee is returned to the starting team, which throws it again. If the opposing team misses the Frisbee, the point is awarded to the starting team. The opposing team then throws the Frisbee. Each team's turn is two throws for an agreed-upon number of rounds.

3. Girls divide into groups of four to six players. The members of each group stand side by side in a line. One girl from each group is chosen to be the leader. The leader stands in front of her group at a distance of ten to fifteen feet. The leader throws the Frisbee to each member of her group. The girls return the Frisbee to the leader in turn. If a girl misses the Frisbee, she has to go to the end of the line. If the leader misses the Frisbee on return, she has to go to the end of the line and the next girl takes her place.

Hoop-to-Hoop Relay

You need: A plunger and ten paper plates with the centers cut out for each team.

How to play: A plunger is placed ten feet or more in front of each team. The game leader stands by to retrieve paper plates and keep score. This is a file relay. The first player on each team tries to throw the ten paper plate rings onto the plunger, one at a time. Then the second players on each team take their turn, and so on. The team with the most points wins.

Lotto Boards

You need: Cardboard, tagboard, or heavy paper; small pictures of plants, animals, natural objects, or common household objects; glue; clear contact paper to cover the board for reuse.

How to make: Cut your lotto board to a desired size and divide into equal-sized squares, using a ruler and pencil. Paste a picture of a different object in each square. When making lotto boards in a troop or group, girls can make boards that are the same or different. Boards can be made specific for a site or experience, such as things found indoors, outdoors, or in a school.

How to play: Each girl or group of girls is given a lotto board. (The lotto board can be one that she makes for herself, or can be one made by another girl.) The goal is to find the objects represented on the board and circle them on the board. If a washable pen is used, the board can be reused.

You need: A plywood board, eight inches square, ½-inch thick; ruler; markers; nine checkers, chips, or buttons, one inch in diameter.

How to make: Mark nine intersecting points on the board, as shown, and draw a circle at each point. Number chips from one through nine.

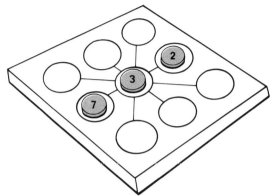

How to play:

Game 1: Girls use chips numbered one through seven. Then place them on circles in lines so that the numbers of the chips in any line add up to 12. The circles to the left and right of the center circle cannot be used.

Game 2: Girls use chips numbered one through nine. Divide them between two players. One girl is given the odd-numbered chips and the other is given the even-numbered chips.

The girl with the odd-numbered chips begins the game by placing one chip in any of the nine circles on the board. The girl with the even-numbered chips next places a chip in any circle she chooses. The first girl to complete a line of three chips that add up to 12 is the winner.

⌂ ◼ ● ⊕ *Maori Stick Game, or Lemmi Sticks*

The Maori stick game began with the Maori people of New Zealand. In the United States, Girl Scouts often call the game lemmi sticks.

You need: Two 12- to 15-inch wooden dowels (1–1½ inches circumference) or a broomstick for each girl; a handsaw; sandpaper; markers, paint, or varnish.

How to make: Cut the dowels or broomsticks to the right length, if necessary. Sand off rough edges and decorate as desired.

How to play: Lemmi sticks is a rhythmic game. Start out with girls seated cross-legged, or kneeling on their heels, facing a partner. Sticks should be held in an upright manner, in the middle of the stick, unless executing a flip or a lengthwise tap. For the flip and lengthwise tap, the sticks should be held at the base, like drumsticks. Girls should be seated close enough to tap each other's sticks, with arms extended. When girls get more experienced, they may desire to work in groups of three or four. The game can also be played seated in a large circle, with opportunities for interesting passing routines.

There are five basic movements:

Clapping: moving two sticks together and striking them.
Tapping: hitting one end of the stick on the ground.
Drumming: hitting one end of the stick, when extended, against the ground or another stick.
Flipping: tossing a stick in the air, turning it once, and catching the other end.
Throwing: throwing the stick to a partner with an upward motion so it is easily caught.

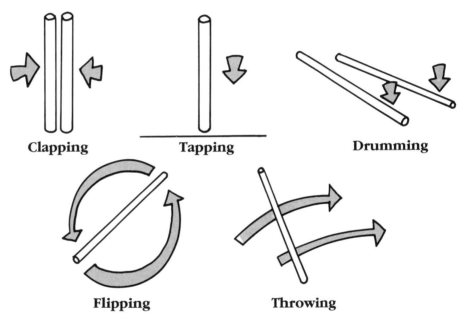

Clapping   **Tapping**   **Drumming**

Flipping   **Throwing**

A *single throw* is when each player throws the same-side stick directly across for an exchange; a *double throw* is when one player throws both sticks to the inside for the other player to catch, and her partner throws both her sticks to the outside for her partner to catch.

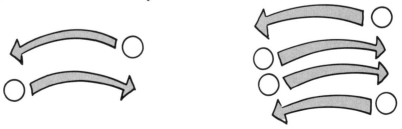

The following are suggested variations, followed by some possible combinations:

- Clapping one or both partner's sticks, directly opposite your stick.
- Clapping sticks on the diagonal.
- Drumming the sticks on the floor in front with one or both sticks.
- Drumming the floor on one side or both sides, with one or both sticks.
- Flipping one or both sticks in the air and catching them, in front or to the side.
- Flipping one or both sticks to a partner, directly across or on the diagonal.

Sample routines:

- Tap sticks on floor in front; clap sticks together in front; tap sticks on floor; clap partner's sticks; tap sticks on floor two times. Drum sticks to both sides on floor; drum sticks together in front; tap sticks on floor in front; drum sticks to both sides on floor; drum sticks together in front; tap sticks on floor in front.
- Clap sticks together in front; exchange sticks with partner, using a single throw; tap on floor in front; clap sticks together in front; exchange sticks with partner using a double throw; tap on floor in front.
- Tap sticks in front; drum sticks to both sides on the floor; flip sticks in air on both sides and catch; drum to the sides; tap sticks in front.

"Titi-Torea" is a song that the Maori sing with the stick game. The words and music follow. When using a song or chant with the stick game, each stick movement is done to a beat of the song. (Girls might enjoy making up their own song or chant.)

Titi-Torea:[6]

E papa wai rangi taku nei mahi
Taku nei mahi he taku ro-mata
E pap wai rangi taku nei mahi
Taku nei manhi he taku ro-mata

E aue ka mate au
E hine hoki iho ra

Maku E kaute o hi-koi tanga
Maku E kaute o hi-koi tanga

E aue ka mate au
E hine hoki iho ra

Huri, huri, huri, huri, o manhara e
Ki te whai, ki te whai i te tau e
Kou rawa kou rawa o mahara e
Kia koe ra e hie. Kia koe ra e hie

"Mock kōw wāy oh ee kōwee taana"

---

[6]Adapted from the arrangement by Hemi Piripata. Copyright Charles Begg and Company, New Zealand.

Titi-Torea

Maori vowels are pronounced like Latin vowels:
a as in father   e as in they   i as in machine   o as in hope   u as in ruby.

Parachute Jump

You need: A handkerchief or square cloth; four pieces of string about eight inches long; a wooden thread spool.

How to make: Tie one string to each corner of the handkerchief. Gather the opposite ends of the four strings together and thread them through the spool. Make a knot so that the four strings are tied together and unable to slip through the spool, as shown. Girls can decorate spools and parachutes.

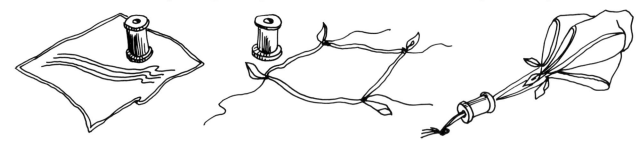

How to play: Have the group determine a parachute jump area and target. Each girl tosses her parachute into the air. The winner is the girl whose parachute lands closest to the target.

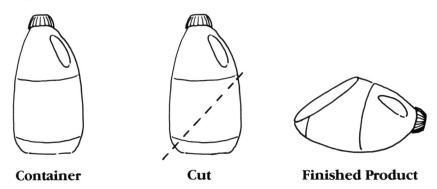

Scooper Ball

You need: A one-gallon plastic bottle with a handle for each girl. A small ball or paper wad for each girl. A pair of scissors.

How to make: Cut plastic bottle as illustrated. Younger girls may need some assistance from the leader in starting the cut. Bottles can be decorated with paint or felt markers.

| **Container** | **Cut** | **Finished Product** |

Girls try the following with the scooper:

- Girls practice throwing a ball into the air and catching it with the scooper. Girls try to do this five times without a miss. Have a contest to see who can do it the most times in a row.
- Standing in a circle or in a group, girls toss the ball around, using the scoopers. See how many times the ball can be passed around without being dropped.
- Girls set up a "scooper ball" court with boundaries and a string or rope running down the middle of the court. Girls divide into two teams and make up rules for a "scooper ball" form of volleyball. Decide what teams must do to score points, how many assists are allowed for each side, and how many points a team must make to win the game.

Variation: Using a sharp object, a girl or adult makes a small hole in the bottom of the bottle. Attach an empty thread spool or a paper wad to one end of a string, running the other through the bottom of the bottle from the outside. Tie a knot in the end of the string so that it will not slip through the hole. The string should be long enough to allow the spool to land in the open end of the bottle. (See illustration.) Holding the handle of the bottle, flip the bottle so that the spool lands in the open end of the bottle.

HOPSCOTCH

Hopscotch is a game popular with children around the world. Although the rules may vary from country to country, the advancement of a player through numbered squares to a goal remains a common objective.

You need: A flat surface that can be marked with chalk, a marker for each girl (for example, a small rock, bottle cap, or old shoe), a hopscotch diagram.

How to play: Girls line up to play. If a girl's marker lands on the line or in the wrong box, her turn is forfeited. Depending upon the specific game, a girl might hop, skip, or jump on one or two feet, with eyes closed, eyes open, hands on head, hands behind back, or in a squatting position.

Hopscotch diagrams are usually copied with chalk on an asphalt or cement playground or sidewalk. Individual blocks in a diagram may vary in size and shape, but they should always be large enough for a girl to stand with both feet in the block. Girls can designate one block a rest area, where players can stop, catch their breath, and stand with both feet on the ground.

The following are representative hopscotch games from around the world. They can be adapted to suit your group.

 *Earth, Water, and Sky*

How to play: The first player stands in the "earth," or "enter," block and tosses her marker into block #1. She must hop on one foot from that block to block #1, pick up her marker and hop back to the earth block. She then tosses her marker into block #2. Hopping to block #2, she picks up her marker and hops back to the earth block. She continues in the same manner through to the ninth block on the diagram. If her marker lands on a wrong square, or if she steps on a line, she must go to the end of the line.

After reaching block nine, she must toss the marker into "sky." If the marker lands on "water," the girl must go to the end of the line. If it lands in "sky," she must hop there, pick up the block and toss it into block nine, continuing play in reverse. If the marker lands on one of the sections marked "bird," she must stand in "sky" and toss her marker over her shoulder with her back to "water." The square where her marker lands is marked with the girl's initials. Other girls cannot jump in that square, but the girl who owns it may use it as a rest square during her turn. If the marker does not land in a square, she loses the opportunity to claim a square. She then continues play in reverse. A winner is determined by finish or ownership of the most squares.

Sharks! Hopscotch

How to play: Girls line up. The first girl tosses her marker. She must hop on one leg three times around the watercourse without stopping. If her marker or foot falls in the area marked "water," she is eaten by sharks and out of the game. If the marker falls on a line or is not in the appropriate square, she loses her turn. Three "island" rest areas are indicated by the letter "I."

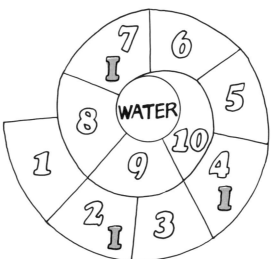

Variation: The first girl to land on an island stakes her claim by writing her initial on the square. No other player can rest there.

You need: A stack of math flash cards for the multiplication tables. This can be a commercial set or an assortment that the girls make before the game using paper and markers.

How to play: One girl draws a flash card to read. The jumper must hop from one block to the next, as dictated by the player reading the card. If she jumps to the proper squares, including the answer squares, she receives a point. The next player then follows a different flash card. Winners can be determined on a points basis.

1	2	3	+	—
0	5	4	9	÷
7	8	6	×	clear
OFF			ON	

For example, if a flash card reads 6 × 8 = ?, the girl does the following:

· She jumps onto the "on" square to start the calculator.
· She then jumps to the "6" square, the "times" square, and the "8" square.
· From the "8" square, she must jump to the answer square (s), in this case, the "4" and the "8" squares.
· Finally she jumps to the "off" square and her turn is complete.
· If a player makes a mistake, she can jump to the "clear" square and start over.

STRING GAMES

String games are found in many cultures around the world. All you need is some string!

You need: Two yards of soft, pliable string or cord, fastened into a circle with a square knot as shown.

How to make: A string weaver uses her thumbs, index, middle, ring, and little fingers. When making the following figures, the strands of strings nearest to the body are referred to as "near strings," strands or loops farthest from the body are referred to as "far strings." A string in front of the palm is called a "palmar string."

Beginning position. Holding the hands so that the palms face each other, make a loop, hooking it behind the thumb and little finger of each hand and passing across the palms.

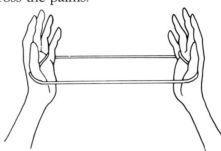

Step 1. The right index finger picks up the left palmar string from underneath. While moving the hands apart, turn the index finger to twist the loop a few times.

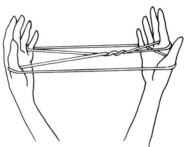

Step 2. The left index finger, from below, picks up the string crossing the right palm from between the strings on the right index loop.

Step 3: Move the hands apart, and release the right thumb and little finger. This is the fishing spear! The right index finger holds the handle of the spear. The left thumb, index, and little finger hold the points. This figure is a popular one among some Native American tribes.

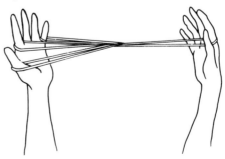

Beginning position. Place the loop behind the thumb, across the palm and behind the little finger of each hand. Pull them apart.

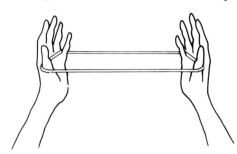

Step 1. The right index finger goes under the left palmar string. Spread the fingers and pull the string back. Do the same with the other hand. This is the "cat's cradle."

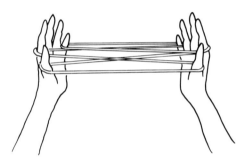

Step 2. The string is freed from both thumbs. The far little finger string is picked up on the backs of the thumbs by reaching under with both thumbs. The thumbs then go back to their original position.

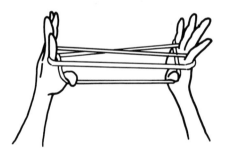

Step 3. Place the thumbs over the near index strings. Pick up the far index strings on the backs of the thumbs.

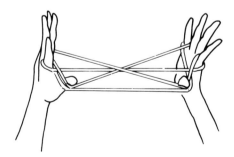

Step 4. Free the little fingers. Place the little fingers over the closest strings. Then pick up the next string on the backs of the little fingers, which go back to their original position.

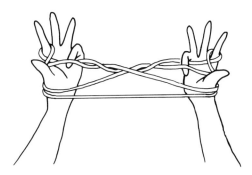

Step 5. Release the thumbs. Cat's whiskers are formed! But do not stop here. . . .

Step 1. Once the cat's whiskers are created, place the thumbs over both index strings. The near little finger string is picked up on the back of the thumbs. The thumbs go back to the original position.

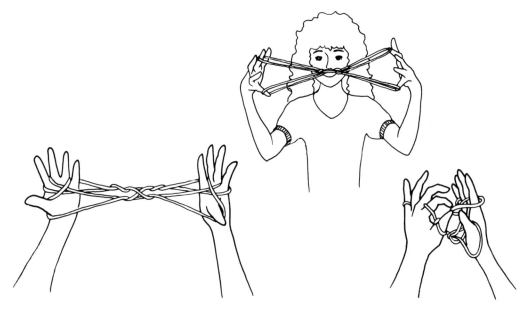

Step 2. Use the right thumb and index finger to pick up the left near index string. Put the string over the left thumb. Use the right thumb and index finger to raise the lower left near thumb string over the string just shifted and let it go. Do the same for the other hand.

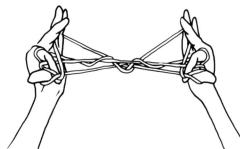

Step 3. Place each index finger from above into the small triangle formed by the palmar string, twisting around the thumb loop. Turn the palms downward. The little fingers let go of the string. Spread the fingers and move the hands apart to make the strings taut. Jacob's ladder is now complete.

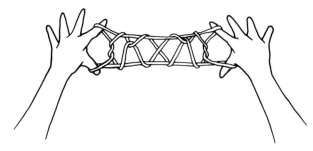

Once Jacob's ladder is created, have a partner help create farmer's pants and suspenders. She places her two index fingers in the two points on either side of the middle bottom triangle and gently pulls down on the two points. Release the thumbs as she is doing this.

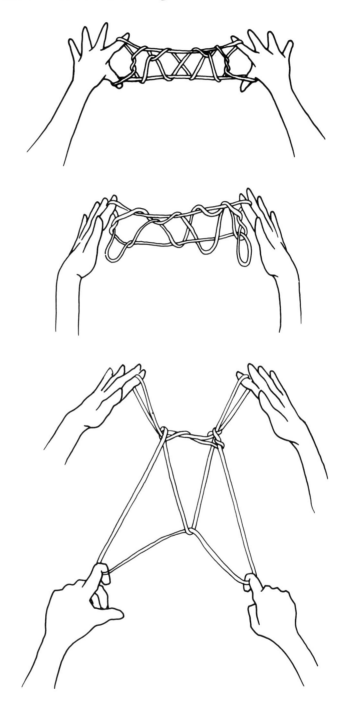

CHAPTER 8

GIRL SCOUT LORE AND SKILLS

GIRL SCOUT LORE

Girl Scout Baseball

You need: A set of numbered questions, each written on a separate slip of paper. A list of correct answers for the umpire. (These questions can be based upon Girl Scout program materials.)

How to play: Four bases and a pitcher's box are marked out. The group is divided into two teams. The game is played like baseball except that instead of throwing a ball, the pitcher draws a question from a hat and "throws" it to the player at bat. If the batter is unable to answer, she may ask the pitcher the same question. If the pitcher fails, the batter takes her base on balls. (No strikes allowed.) If the batter answers correctly, she runs to first base. If she does not know the correct answer and the pitcher does, the batter is out. If the second batter answers correctly, the first batter runs to second base. After a question is "thrown," the umpire counts to ten. Any member of the opposing team may "catch" the ball by answering correctly after the batter has had her chance. Three "outs" retires the side. Each player who reaches home scores one run.

Girl Scout Promise Relay

You need: The words of the Girl Scout Promise and Law printed on cards, one word on each card. One complete set of cards for each team. (Each set is mixed up, put into a box or envelope, and placed on a table about ten feet in front of each team.)

How to play: Use a file relay formation. On signal, No. 1 players run to the table, select the cards containing the words of the first line of the Girl Scout Promise, and place them in order on the table. When finished, each girl returns and tags her player No. 2, who runs to the table. If there is an error in the order of the words for the first line, player No. 2 corrects it before selecting words for the second line of the Promise and placing them in correct order. The game continues until one team completes the Promise and Law. If there are less than 15 players to a team, at least one girl will participate twice.

Girl Scout Riddle

You need: A blackboard and chalk, or pencils and a pad of paper for each team.

How to play: Divide the group into teams. On the blackboard or paper pad, each team prints the words "GIRL SCOUTS" in a vertical position. The object is for each team to fill in the Girl Scout Law horizontally so that each letter in the vertical line becomes a letter in the horizontal line, with the exception of the first line, "I will do my best." For example:

I will do my best:
- to show respect for myself and others throu**G**h my words and actions
- to be fa**I**r
- to help whe**R**e I am needed
- to be cheerfu**L**
- to be a **S**ister to every Girl Scout
- to respe**C**t authority
- to be h**O**nest
- to protect and improve the world aro**U**nd me
- to be friendly and considera**T**e
- to use resources wi**S**ely

The team that finishes first wins. There are many possible variations.

Girl Scouts Are Great!

You need: Paper and pencil for each girl.

How to play: Have each girl print the sentence "Girl Scouts are great!" or a similar sentence at the top of her paper. Ask each girl to find as many different words as she can using the letters in the sentence in a timed period. Letters can only be used as many times as they appear in the sentence.

Handbook Treasure Hunt

You need: Girl Scout handbook for each pair of girls, paper, and pencils. The leader has a list of items to look for.

How to play: Divide girls into pairs. Each pair of girls receives a list of ten things to find in the book. They must write down the page number where each item is located. The first pair to finish are the winners. Share and discuss the results. For example, the following are some items from the *Junior Girl Scout Handbook:* a song, a ceremony, the Girl Scout Promise, a game, a camping skill, a craft, a safety tip, something that helps the environment, a form of troop government.

Variation: *Safety-Wise* might be used for older girls.

International Kim's Game

You need: At least nine objects from other WAGGGS countries, four long sticks or pieces of string that can be laid out to make a tic-tac-toe grid, and a towel or blanket that will cover everything. Pencils and paper for each player.

How to play: Place each object from another country in a square of the grid. Cover before the girls come into the room. Explain that an opportunity will be given to view nine different objects from nine countries that have Girl Guides and Girl Scouts. Remove the cover for approximately two minutes. After viewing, they should list or draw each of the objects. Discuss what each object is made of, what it might be used for, and what information the object might provide about the country of origin.

New Zealand Game

This game was presented to Girl Scouts of the U.S.A. from Girl Guides in New Zealand.

You need: Slips of paper with the name of a badge or parts of the Girl Scout Law written on each one. Pencil and paper for each player, magazines, and newspapers.

How to play: Divide girls into pairs. Each pair is given a folded slip of paper. Within a specified time, each pair must find pictures representing the message written on its slip of paper. For example, "A Girl Scout is loyal" can be represented by a picture of an American flag and two friends together. The World of Today and Tomorrow Dabbler can be represented by a computer, a telescope, and recycling. Each pair groups its pictures for display and is given a number to post at the display. All pairs then jot down the numbers of the displayed items and try to guess the message each group of pictures represents. The pair who correctly guesses the most messages wins.

 *We Belong*

This is a game that can be played after a troop has learned about the World Association of Girl Guides and Girl Scouts.

You need: A current list of all the member countries of the World Association of Girl Guides and Girl Scouts. (A WAGGGS list is available to Girl Scout leaders through their councils.)

How to play: The group is seated in circle formation and players are numbered consecutively. The odd numbers compete with the even numbers. The game leader calls one odd and one even number, then counts three seconds. The first player to name a country belonging to the World Association of Girl Guides and Girl Scouts scores one point for her team. The winning team is the one that first scores ten points.

Variation: If a globe or world map is available, the game can be made more challenging by requiring each girl to name and locate a country. Score two points when both are done correctly. The team with the higher score wins.

OUTDOOR SKILLS

 *Blindfold Test*

You need: Blindfolds and practice rope for each pair of girls.

How to play: Divide girls into pairs. One girl is blindfolded, and her partner names a knot to tie and times her. Girls reverse roles.

Boil, Water, Boil

You need: Matches, pots or empty coffee cans, water, tinder and kindling supply, fire safety equipment (bucket of water and shovel), fireplace or fire ring.

How to play: On signal, each team searches for the sizes of wood essential to build a small fire. Teams return to a selected site; each team builds a fire and sets a pot of water on it. The first team to boil water wins. (Be sure to stress safety and minimal impact.)

Variation: Burn, fire, burn. Suspend a string horizontally (about three-feet high) over an area where two fires can be built. Girls work in two teams to see who burns through the string first using tinder and kindling.

You need: Two decks of 3″ × 5″ index cards with each of the 32 points of the compass on them. (You may only want to do 8 or 16, depending on the group.) A judge to watch the circles.

N, S, E, W are the cardinal points of the compass.

NE, SE, SW, NW are the ordinal points of the compass.

Next come: NNE, ENE, ESE, SSE, SSW, WSW, WNW, and NNW.

Lastly: N by NNE, NE by NNE, NE by ENE, E by ENE, E by ESE, SE by ESE, SE by SSE, S by SSE, S by SSW, SW by SSW, SW by WSW, W by WSW, W by WNW, NW by WNW, NW by NNW, N by NNW.

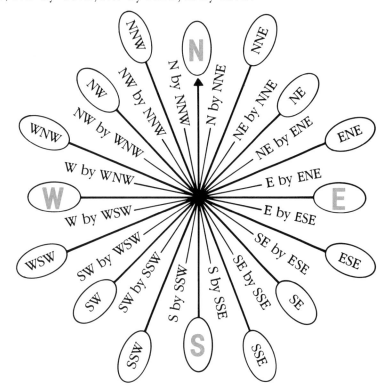

How to play: Demonstrate the compass rose to the girls by laying down the cards in order in a circle, starting with N at the top of the circle. Divide the group into two teams, each with a shuffled deck of cards. Teams line up in file formation and player No. 1 takes the first card and runs to the designated area where she lays it down in an imaginary circle. She runs back to tag player No. 2, who takes the next card and lays it in the proper position in the circle. This goes on until the compass rose is complete. If a card is placed incorrectly, the next girl must put it in its right place, before taking a new card. **Note:** The game can be simplified by using only the first 16 points of the compass rose.

Variation: Time individuals or teams.

Compass Hunt

You need: A compass for each girl or team, paper, and pencil. For this game, girls must know how to use the compass and how to use pace to determine distance.

How to play: Each team is charged with laying a compass trail for the other team. They should give degree readings and paces or distances from one station to the next. When teams have laid their trails, have them follow each other's trail.

Variation: Lay the trail for the group beforehand with clues and a treasure at the end.

Hiking Equipment Relay

You need: Pencil and paper for each team.

How to play: Divide the group into teams of equal size. Write as many numbers on each sheet of paper as there are girls on each team. On a signal, each No. 1 runs to her team's sheet of paper and writes down an item that the group will need on a hike. She then runs back and touches her team's No. 2 player. Items may not be repeated. (Girl Scout handbooks and *Safety-Wise* are good resources in case of ties and for a discussion afterward.)

Knot Relay

You need: A piece of rope for each team, a list of knots girls can tie, a short stick (for such knots as the clove hitch).

How to play: Divide into teams of equal size and count off. Each team sits or stands in a circle, with the No. 1 player holding the piece of rope. At a given signal, along with announcing the name of the knot, the No. 1 player runs around the circle and returns to her place. She must then tie the knot correctly. She passes the rope to the player on her left, who must untie the knot before starting around the circle. Each girl takes a turn until the rope has come back to the No. 1 player and she has untied the knot. The game leader can announce a different knot to be tied.

Sealed Orders

You need: Written sealed orders based on the current interests of the group; items needed to carry out the orders. Orders are written by the game leader in advance.

How to play: The group is divided into teams, each with a captain. Each team numbers off and is given a name and its sealed orders. On a signal, the captains open the orders and the teams begin to carry them out. The No. 1 player carries out the No. 1 order, and so on. As each order is carried out, the player reports to the captain of her team. The team that finishes its orders first wins. For example, orders for ten girls with a backpack tent: 1) Select a tent site. 2) Roll out tent. 3) Put together poles. 4) Put in tent pegs. 5) Put in tent pegs. 6) Help stand up tent. 7) Help stand up tent. 8) Put on tent fly. 9) Put on tent fly. 10) Pretend you are hitting the hay!

Variation: Carry out sealed orders without talking.

Simon Says: Knots

You need: A three-foot length of rope for each participant, a list of knots everyone knows, and a leader.

How to play: Every time "Simon says" to tie a certain knot, each girl must do it. If the command doesn't start with "Simon says," girls do nothing. A girl misses if she ties the knot incorrectly, ties the wrong knot, or ties one at the wrong time. After three misses, a girl is out.

Troop Camping Menu Planning

You need: Several large grocery bags, paper, pencils, outdoor cookbooks.

How to play: Label grocery bags "breakfast," "lunch," "dinner," "snacks"; or "main dish," "vegetable," "fruit," "dessert," "beverage," or a combination to fit the group's needs. Have each girl put two slips of paper into each bag, one with a favorite food from the category, the other with a new dish she would like to try. Menus can be made up by drawing slips out of the bag.

Variation: Label the bags "one pot," "fireless," "camp stove," "solar," to get some variety in cooking skills.

CHAPTER 9

NATURE AWARENESS GAMES

WHY NATURE AWARENESS GAMES?

Nature awareness games are used to learn about nature. They can be fun for all ages and also contain important lessons about biological interrelationships, basic ecological principles, and the classification of plants and animals. Games can be a way to enjoy the outdoors, learn to use different senses, and sharpen observation skills. Nature games may be a child's first exposure to the outdoors in a nonthreatening, supportive environment.

There are a few things to keep in mind when introducing nature games to a group:

- Set the stage. If you are introducing an environmental concept, determine how the game relates to the concept and use examples that girls are familiar with. If you are using a process such as classification or identification, make sure that girls understand the process by reviewing the process before playing the game.
- Think minimal impact. Don't pick plants, tamper with or remove animals from homes, waste food, or cause damage to a site. Involve girls in determining how to promote this ethic in games.
- Plan a debriefing session after each nature game. Relate the game to the concepts introduced. For example, if playing toothpick barnyard bedlam, the goal is not just to pick up toothpicks of different colors, but to relate the colors to the concepts of camouflage and predator-prey relationships. Ask questions to generate discussion and to determine if concepts are linked in girls' minds.

NATURE HIKES

Alphabet Hike

You need: Paper and pencil for each team.

How to play: Divide hikers into teams, each with a captain. Any player from either team who sees something beginning with the letter "a" that pertains to nature names it, and her team captain writes it down. Members of that team then look for something beginning with "b." The team wins that gets furthest through the alphabet before the hike ends.

Variations: Have teams or individuals search for things beginning with letters in any order. Have teams or individuals search for plants only, animals only, or combinations.

Nature Lotto

You need: Lotto game boards (see page 73) made with nature pictures, marking pens.

How to play: When hiking, have girls look for objects on their nature lotto boards. The game can be played like bingo, with five squares filled in in any direction, or with all the squares filled in on the board.

See It Hike

How to play: One girl starts the game by naming something that she sees as the group is walking. "I see a bird." The next person must call out something that she sees that begins with a "d", the last letter of the first word called out. "I see a daisy." The next person calls out something that begins with a "y" and so forth. The group can decide whether to allow multiple words or adjectives, such as "yellow flower."

Other Kinds of Nature Hikes

There are many different things and combinations of activities one can do on a hike. The kind of hike, its length, and activities should be geared to the girls and their experience. Hikes can be fun as well as a way to use the senses and learn more about the world around us. Here are some suggestions that are Girl Scout favorites:

- **Color chip hike.** Match paint samples or colored paper chips to natural colors as you are hiking.
- **Clothing color hike.** Find colors in nature to match colors in items of clothing worn by each girl.
- **Penny hike.** Toss a coin at each opportunity for a turn to determine the direction to hike.
- **Smaller-than-a-penny hike.** Find things that are smaller than a penny on your hike.
- **Scent hike.** Use bottled scents (like vanilla) or an onion to lay a trail for the group to follow.
- **Seed hike.** Look for different kinds of seeds and how they travel.
- **Throwaway art hike.** Collect nonliving things in the palm of the hand to arrange a special design or picture. Share your creation and toss it back on the ground. (Avoid littering.)
- **Track hike.** Look for different kinds of tracks and animal signs during the hike.

NATURE LESSONS

Animal Call Out

How to play: The group forms a circle; one player is "it." "It" calls out "amphibian," "bird," "fish," "mammal," or "reptile," and points to one of the players and starts counting from one to ten. The player tries to name a creature in the group that was called out before "it" finishes counting. If a player fails, she becomes "it." Discuss the things that these creatures have in common. Discuss what makes them different.

Animal Who Am I?

You need: A picture of an animal species for each person and safety pins or masking tape. An alternative is to make a set of pictures mounted on cardboard with string attached to go around each girl's neck. Before playing this game, the game leader should discuss questioning strategies with the girls. Brainstorm types of questions that can be asked to classify an animal, such as where it lives, how it moves, the kind of food it eats, whether it has fur, feathers or scales, etc. With younger girls, hold up each picture and have the girls discuss the animals prior to play.

How to play: Place a picture on each girl's back, where others can see it, but she cannot. She must ask questions about the picture that can be answered by a "yes" or "no." A limit can be set on the number of questions per person. After girls have guessed their animals, lead the group in a discussion about animal families. Ask girls to arrange themselves in groups of related species or in habitat groups. Discuss the different combinations.

Bird Relay

Relay form: File.

You need: A set of bird pictures and a set of bird descriptions for each team. Prior to playing, discuss identifying characteristics to look for when identifying a bird. A bird book can be helpful in doing this.

How to play: The pictures of the birds are posted at the front of the room or placed on a table. Teams stand in file formation. The No. 1 players are each given a written description of a bird. On signal, they read the descriptions and search for the bird pictures that match the descriptions. They take the pictures, return to their teams, and tag the next player in line. The winning team has the largest number of correct matches.

Variation: This relay can also be played using pictures and descriptions of plants, animals, or other categories.

Food Chain Lineup

You need: A set of 3″ × 5″ index cards with the names of plants and animals from your surroundings written on each card, one per card. Include one sun card.

How to play: Pass out a card to each person. Explain that in a food chain each creature is dependent upon something else for its food. For example:

SUN < GRASS < COW < VULTURE

Girls make a food chain by standing in back of and placing their hands on the shoulders of the girl who represents a food source.

Do the preceding example and then ask the group to create their own food chains. Ask them to form the longest food chain they can and the shortest.

Variation: When the group understands the food chain concept, have them do a food chain lap-sit. While standing close together and grasping the shoulders of the person in front of her, each player must sit back on the lap of the person behind her, balancing the group. Ask or demonstrate what happens when one part of a food chain is destroyed.

Food Web Game

You need: A ball of string; a card for each girl with a name of an animal, plant, or natural resource found in an ecosystem being studied.

How to play: Give each girl a card with the name of an animal, plant, or resource (such as water, sun, soil). This game works best with a minimum of ten and a maximum of 20 players. Have the "sun girl" start the game off by taking the ball of string and passing it to a girl whose card she directly affects, such as a plant. The "plant" then passes the string to something she directly affects or is affected by, such as a "cow," and so forth. If the group is large, do not pass the string to each girl more than once. If it is a smaller group, pass the string to girls as often as possible, without repeating direct relationships. At the end, when the web is evident, have the girls discuss how many things are affected by one element in the food web. This can be shown by having one girl pull on all of her strings and having girls who feel the pull raise their free hand. (Do not let go.) Ask what happens when there is a drought? a forest fire? when chemicals are put into the soil?

Sample cards for a forest ecosystem: fir tree, fern, slug, woodpecker, squirrel, spider, mosquito, fox, mouse, soil, sun, water.

Sample cards for a pond ecosystem: water, sun, frog, tadpole, fish, duckweed, mallard, water beetle, planaria, snail, kingfisher, algae.

Owls and Crows[7]

You need: A playing field with a centerline and a home-base line behind each team.

How to play: Divide the group into two teams, the Owls and the Crows. They must face each other several feet apart with the centerline between them. The leader calls out a statement such as "All green plants need the sun" to the group. If it is true, the Owls chase the Crows, attempting to tag them before they reach their home base. If it is false, the Crows chase the Owls. If a girl is caught, she joins the team that caught her. Statements can be about things that are observed in the outdoors, about concepts that have been discussed, or about points of identification. If there is confusion around an answer, the leader should give the correct answer. This game is good for reinforcing nature awareness and concepts.

USING THE SENSES

Back-to-Back

You need: A pencil and paper or a 3″ × 5″ index card for each pair of girls. An assorted collection of interesting natural objects, such as feathers, cones, rocks, bones, seedpods.

How to play: Have girls sit back-to-back on the ground. One girl has the pencil and paper, while the other has an object unseen by her partner. The girl holding the object must describe the object in detail, without telling her partner what it is. This game provides a good opportunity for scientific observation skills and demonstrates the importance of good description. Have the girls compare their drawings with the objects. Then have them trade places and play the game again with new objects.

---

[7]Joseph Bharat Cornell, *Sharing Nature with Children.* Nevada City, Calif: Ananda Publications, 1979.

Making Tracks

You need: Animal track resource books, a card with the name of an animal printed on it for each team, a station with sandy soil for each group.

How to play: Divide the group into teams. Give each team a number. Each team is given an animal track book and a card with an animal's name. The teams each go to a station where they can create animal tracks for their animal in the sand. When all the groups are finished, assemble at the first group's tracks. Each team should write down the name of the animal it thinks made the tracks. After touring the stations, the teams should announce what animals they were assigned. This process can be repeated. Discuss where tracks might be observed in the area, and what kind of animals might be making these tracks. If possible, look for real animal tracks on a hike.

Nature Scavenger Hunt

You need: Scavenger hunt list, defined boundaries.

How to play: This scavenger hunt does not emphasize collecting. Rather, girls record and describe each object as it is found. Girls can do the scavenger hunt as individuals, as pairs, or in a group while hiking. The game leader can set a time limit if it is a contest, or tell girls to take their time discovering things along the hike. The following is a sample scavenger hunt list:

- The largest thing
- The smallest thing
- Something yellow
- The coolest place
- The hottest place
- An eroded trail
- The oldest item
- The newest item
- The prettiest thing
- Something with six legs
- A seed
- Something that has no place in nature
- A compound leaf
- Something round
- Something important in nature
- Something soft
- Something hard
- A chewed leaf
- Something perfectly straight
- Something that makes a noise
- A camouflaged animal or insect
- Something that changed the environment
- A sun trap (this could be a rock or a green leaf, for example)

Rattlers[8]

You need: Two things that can be used as rattles, such as coffee cans with lids with gravel inside, and two blindfolds.

How to play: Have the group form a circle with two blindfolded players inside the circle. Each has a rattle. One player is the chased, while the other is the chaser. The object is for the chaser to catch the chased. When one player rattles, the other must answer back immediately; however, the chaser can initiate the rattle by shaking only five times during the game. The chased can rattle as much as she wants to find out where the chaser is. The group forming the circle can keep the rattlers in bounds and offer encouragement. They can also change from a circle to another shape. This game can lead into a discussion of snakes and the use of the senses in predator-prey relationships.

Search and Sketch

You need: Pencils and crayons, clipboards or cardboard to draw on, a chart or worksheet with directions for girls, or a list girls can copy.

How to play: There are many variations to a search and sketch. The game leader needs to pick a safe site for the activity, and set boundaries and time limits. This can be an activity for pairs. Explain that this is like a scavenger hunt, but that girls are to sketch what they find on the paper provided. Here are some sample topics:

- Find two signs of the current season.
- Locate four sources of water or air pollution. Draw pictures of them and list what you think can be done about them.
- Find a place to sit for a few minutes. Listen for sounds and draw a picture of what you think might be making the sounds.
- Search for three natural materials used by people and draw pictures of them and how they are used.
- Find three things that are food for wildlife. Draw the animals you think eat these things.

Sound Maps

You need: Paper or 3″ × 5″ index card and pencil for each girl.

How to play: Ask each girl to find a special place to sit outdoors. Before the girls find their places, have them place an "X" in the middle of their papers to represent themselves. As they listen, have them map the different sounds that they hear around them, using symbols to represent the sound. At the end of the time allotted, have them share their maps and discoveries.

---

[8]Excerpt from the *New Games Book,* by Andrew Fluegelman, copyright 1976 by the Headlands Press, Inc. Used by permission of Doubleday, a division of Bantam, Doubleday, Dell Publishing Group, Inc.

Toothpick Barnyard Bedlam

You need: 100 toothpicks, 25 each of four different colors (blue, yellow, green, red); a paper bag for each group. Scatter the toothpicks in a designated area, such as a large meadow or playing field.

How to play: This is a game about camouflage. It is a noisy game for large groups of people. Divide the group into teams. Each group represents an animal, and must practice making its animal's noise. Each team must select a captain, who carries the team's paper bag. Explain the boundaries of the search. Caution the group to beware of sharp toothpicks in the grass. At a signal, the total group rushes out to the area seeded with toothpicks. When a toothpick is discovered, a player must stand and point at it while making her team's animal noise. The team captain is the *only* one who can pick up toothpicks. Have the group gather toothpicks for five minutes. Have each team total up their toothpicks by individual color. Total the toothpicks by color and have the group search again. Play until all the toothpicks are gathered. Debrief the group. Consider such things as which colors of toothpicks were found first, and why, and what kind of behavior was displayed by individuals when toothpick supplies were limited. Ask the girls for some examples of camouflage and competition in the natural world.

The Un-Nature Trail[9]

You need: An assortment of items that wouldn't normally be found outdoors (such as spoons, pots and pans, staplers, litter, rubber ducks). A location that has a trail or path where items can be hung or placed. The leader must set up the trail ahead of time, "salting" the trail with 15–20 items. Keep a list of items and locations for discussion afterward.

How to play: Explain to the group that they are to walk the "un-nature trail" looking for things that do not belong there. Have each girl write down the items she sees without sharing her discoveries. At the end, compare the items found. Before telling where items are, walk the trail again. Then walk the trail, pointing out the items. This activity lends itself to discussions on camouflage, littering, and observational skills.

---

[9]Joseph Bharat Cornell, *Sharing Nature with Children.* Nevada City, Calif.: Ananda Publications, 1979.

CHAPTER 10

WIDE GAMES AND SPECIAL EVENTS

WHAT IS A WIDE GAME?

Wide games have been a part of Girl Guide and Girl Scout program for many years. They are fun and a challenging way to move a large group of people through a series of activities that are tied together by a common theme. They are called wide games because they generally cover a larger area than other games and they usually last longer than other games. In fact, a wide game may last an hour or a day, depending on the objectives and the group.

Wide games are often used to teach or test knowledge or to develop teamwork among girls. They can be competitive or noncompetitive. Generally, they follow a specific theme from station to station, beginning and ending with large group assemblies. The theme helps to pull unrelated activities together (a "rainbow" theme might pull together activities from each of the five worlds of Girl Scouting), or helps determine the activities chosen (a "lost in the wilderness" theme might focus on campcraft skills).

Activities can be from Girl Scout program materials, with recognitions acknowledged, or they can be linked to other girl interests, developmental needs, or community resources. Activities related to the theme can be used during the passage from one station to the next. These might involve decoding a secret message or looking for specific objects along the way.

The development of the wide-game theme can be very simple or can involve a lot of creativity, including make-believe, role-playing, costumes, and secret orders. Make-believe is usually well-received by Daisy and Brownie Girl Scouts. When fantasy is used with Junior Girl Scouts or older girls, an element of humor or role-playing needs to be present. Above all, the development of a theme should add to the fun and spirit of the activity.

STEPS IN PLANNING A WIDE GAME

- Decide who the audience is for the wide game. What are the ages, program levels, interests, abilities, and needs of the girls? How many people are involved? Establish objectives that take all of this into account.
- Determine the planning group and how girls can be involved in the development and presentation of the wide game.
- Select a theme and activities that will tie into the objectives. Decide how many stations are needed, and if there are activities needed between stations. Every station can be active every rotation, or some stations can be idle during some of the rotations. Do not have more groups than activity stations.
- Find a site for the wide game. This might be a camp, a park, a school ground, a large indoor facility, or a neighborhood. Use *Safety-Wise* as a guide, and be sure that there are adequate sanitary and drinking water facilities. Visit the site to finalize the selection.

- Chart a time schedule and flow for group activity. Your total time estimate should include an equal time for each activity period (activities need to be created to happen in the same time span); an opening and closing time period; time for moving between stations; time for any snacks, meals, or breaks; and consideration for the age and abilities of your group.
- Plan the activities for each station. Activities need to stand alone, as groups will be arriving at each activity in a different rotation. Make the props, gather the costumes, and get the materials needed. This can be done by a committee, a troop, or those responsible for the station. Activities can also be planned for the groups to do between stations. If the game is competitive, decide on a scoring system and appoint a judge/arbitrator. Planners who know the game should not be participants.
- Determine who is responsible for the overall logistics, registration (if needed), safety, and leadership. Plan an opening activity and a closing activity to set the tone and to pull it all together.

IDEAS FOR WIDE GAMES AND SPECIAL EVENTS

- Bicycle gymkhana
- Careers
- Contemporary issues
  (e.g., drug education, self-esteem, pluralism)
- Crafts
- Ecology
- Environmental problems/action
- Five worlds of interest
- Folktales
- Games
- Geography
- Getting to know your camp
- Health and fitness
- Hobbies
- Juliette Low's birthday
- Local history
- Multicultural influences
  (e.g., food, dance, games, crafts)
- Music
- Nature at night
- Nature study
- Olympic games
- Outdoor education
- Outdoor skills
- Safety
- Science fair
- Sensory awareness
- Specific holidays
  (avoid ethnic or religious ones)
- Specific Try-Its, badges,
  or interest projects
- Sports
- Swimming skills
- Trail signs
- Thinking Day
- WAGGGS
- Walkathon
- Water activities

GUIDELINES FOR DOING BROWNIE GIRL SCOUT TRY-ITS AND GIRL SCOUT BADGE WIDE GAMES

There are many specific Brownie Girl Scout Try-Its and Junior Girl Scout activities in the five worlds of interest that can be combined to create an effective wide game and provide an introduction to different Try-Its or badges. There are also some Brownie Girl Scout Try-Its and Junior Girl Scout badges that can be completed in the course of a daylong workshop or wide game, with proper planning and resources.

By using these program materials as a base for a wide game, enthusiasm can be generated for earning Try-Its and badges, and giving girls an opportunity to start on or earn a recognition. New or inexperienced leaders will learn new ways to work with girls. Girls who are not in troops can be provided with an opportunity to earn a recognition with other girls.

Badge-earning should be balanced with other aspects of Girl Scout program and the individual or group's need for recognition. Girls and adults often forget that Girl Scout program is more than earning badges, and that in real life one does not always earn quick recognition for experiences or accomplishments. Many Try-Its and badges involve time for investigation, use of outside resources, time to observe change, and mastery of skills. There is also a danger that activities chosen will not be appropriate for everyone in the group, or that they are activities that require more depth and opportunity to gain expertise than the wide-game format allows for.

If you decide to develop a wide game or activity workshop, here are some questions to consider:

- How can girl planning be used? Can girls be in charge of the event? Can girls be in charge of each activity? Can girls choose the Try-It or badge activity?
- Can girl decision-making be built-into the event itself? Can each group elect a leader at the specific activity site? Can the decision-making process be built into the activity? Can girls choose as a group or as individuals which activities they will rotate to? Are there more activities than there is time, so that choices will have to be made?
- Does the event have a variety of age-level and skill-level and interest range activities for the participants?
- Is there a game leader or sealed orders at each station? Is opportunity for teamwork built into each station activity? Is the activity safe?
- Are all the resources provided that are needed for each activity—books, people, equipment, etc?
- Are the activities at each station "hands on"?
- Is enough time allowed for completion or mastery of the chosen activity?

The following are some additional suggestions:

- There may be one or two activities (possibly required ones) that can be done as a total group, such as visiting an ambulance or learning how to give CPR if girls are working on the First-Aid badge.
- Have more stations than there are rotating groups, if possible. Groups can choose their stations on a first-come, first-served basis. Use a timer and a whistle to help move the group.
- Use adults or older girls as facilitators or resource persons during rotational periods, but try to set up stations so that girls will do learning on their own.

ONE MODEL FOR ON-SITE REGISTRATION AND DIVISION OF AN UNKNOWN NUMBER OF PARTICIPANTS

Objectives:
- To make registration for troop and group leaders and the council as simple as possible.
- To shift responsibility for permission slips and collection of money from event leaders or the council to troop leaders.
- To create rotating groups that mix the girls from different troops effectively, so that the event provides an opportunity to make new friends.
- To make each troop responsible for a part of the event.

Each troop or leader must:
- Sign up with the event director by a deadline to let the director know the troop plans to participate. At this time the troop-sponsored activity is accepted and assigned.
- Be responsible for the setup of the sponsored activity or guest speaker.
- Provide one adult or older girl for activity supervision at the troop or group activity station during the event.
- Be responsible for holding troop permission slips, submitting a list of participating girls to the event leader, and paying a set event fee, if needed.
- Provide one adult or older girl to rotate with a rotating group.

To do this for approximately one hundred participants and ten participating troops or groups, numbers can be adjusted as needed:
- The event team needs to prepare ahead of time ten envelopes, ten sets of 12 stickers (each set simple but different, using symbols and colors), and ten sets of 11 self-adhesive name tags, one tag clearly marked adult. Set up the ten envelopes, each one having a different sticker on the outside.

- Place the sets of stickers on the name tags, putting ten girl and one adult one in each envelope.
- Determine where each station will be on your event site. Create a master poster that can be posted at the registration area. It should name each event, assign a symbol, and determine the order of rotation based on a logical flow.
- Mark each station on the site with the symbol and its number in rotation. Include a symbol of the next station in rotation.

To register on-site:
- Someone should be in charge of passing out name tags and keeping track of those passed out.
- Ask one person from each troop to approach the registration area: give her one adult name tag with a symbol, explaining that that person will be expected to stay with the symbol group the whole event. Give her as many girl symbol tags as needed, but not all of one symbol. Give her different symbols in groups of two or three, so that her troop is divided. As the tag is taken from an envelope, tally the tag on the outside of the envelope. In this way the symbol groups can be kept even in numbers.
- Instruct the leader where the first-aid station is, where water and restrooms are, and where the troop is to set up its station. After the station is set up, the troop is to gather for the opening of the wide game.

Group orientation and event hints:
- Start the event and end the event with a friendship circle or other large group gathering. It is a great way to focus attention on the group and one of the objectives of the event.
- Explain to participants that the color and shape of their name tags tell them where they will be starting out in the wide game. Take time to point out where each station is. Also point out that the station markers show where to go for the next rotation. Introduce the adult or leader of each group by symbol and give an opportunity for the group to get together before asking them to go to their first stations.
- Have someone in charge of timing the event. A whistle does wonders in helping with rotation. The timer can walk between the groups to check on stations and give a warning before blowing the whistle, although each station should be a timed activity.

SAMPLE WIDE GAMES

The following are two wide games written for different age levels. One is for Junior Girl Scouts at night; the other is to introduce the worlds of Girl Scouting to Brownie Girl Scouts. These are outlines and do not represent the full range of creativity that can be used when writing the script for each station or traveling between stations. Let the imagination and creativity of the planning group guide the design of the game for the specific audience, needs, and site. Enjoy the results!

Night Walk

Audience: Thirty Junior Girl Scouts

Site: Resident or troop campsite

Objectives:
- To introduce girls to the outdoors at night
- To use all the senses and sharpen observation skills
- To increase the comfort level with night activities
- To have fun

Each girl has a flashlight and her own bandanna for a blindfold. Each group has a compass.

Start the wide game by assembling everyone, setting the tone, and leading the group in a silent walk to the campfire area. Divide the group into teams, giving them secret orders on how to get to their first and last station.

Station 1: The Sky at Night
Have girls find constellations and a planet.

You need: Star chart, telescope, station orders, facilitator, and directions for movement between stations.

Movement between stations 1 and 2:
Follow rope blindfolded from station 1 to station 2. Listen for sounds. Debrief at station 2.

Station 2: Sky Legends
Have the girls sit and talk about sounds they heard. At the station, have an adult (preferably Native American) tell a Native American legend linking sounds and the sky.

You need: Legend teller, directions for movement between stations.

Movement between stations 2 and 3:
The adult or girl at the head of the group carries a flashlight. Follow a rope or trail that has been marked with "wildlife eyes" cut out of reflector tape. Have the group spot the eyes as they walk.

Station 3: Creature Feature
Have girls count the number of insects that are attracted to this station and try to identify some of them, or have someone with a display of nocturnal animals and discuss their habits.

You need: Sheet stretched between trees and light behind the sheet; insect and mammal books; U.S. or state wildlife animal study pelts or possibly a live owl that is from a bird rehabilitation center; directions for movement between stations.

Movement between stations 3 and 4:
Same as between stations 2 and 3, using different eyes.

Station 4: Night Sounds

Debrief the girls on the wildlife eyes that they observed. Have a chart for them to look at. Have the girls sit in a large area and listen for a set amount of time. Ask them to draw a sound map (see page 103). Compare the maps.

You need: Night-eye chart with animal eyes identified; 3″ × 5″ index cards and pencils for each girl. Directions for the movement between stations.

Movement between stations 4 and 5:
Have the girls find the next station by their sense of smell. They must follow a previously laid "onion hike" trail through the woods. (Supply emergency back-up directions in a separate envelope, or provide an observer to keep them from getting lost in the dark.)

Station 5: Touchy Feely

Have the girls try to draw items that they can only feel, or practice describing textures and shapes.

You need: A box with a hand-size hole; objects to insert for touch and feel; directions for movement between stations; and a compass for each group. (**Safety note:** Use safe things for touch that do not hurt or scare girls.)

Movement between stations 5 and 6: Provide a compass and directions to the next station using a given number of paces.

Directions for each group after it has arrived back at the first station: Compass directions and a map to arrive back at the campfire area for s'mores and songs about the night. Each group comes prepared to share one song about the night with the entire group.

 *Follow the Rainbow*

Audience: 50 Brownie Girl Scouts from three schools in same service unit

Site: Park or schoolyard

Objectives:
· To introduce girls to activities in each of the five worlds of interest in Girl Scouting.
· To mix girls from different troops and different schools.
· To have fun.

Girls are divided at registration (see pages 21–22) by six color groups. The total group starts out by making a large circle and singing the "Brownie

Smile Song." They then group in their color groups with a leader and proceed to their starting stations.

Station 1: Orange. "Over the Rainbow," World of Today and Tomorrow. Make a Color Spectrum activity from "Science in Action." (*Brownie Girl Scout Handbook*, page 255).

Between-station action: Girls link arms and sing "We're Off to See the Wizard," skipping to the next station.

Station 2: Blue. "This isn't Kansas, Toto." World of People. "Meeting People" from "Manners" (*Brownie Girl Scout Handbook*, page 214). Build on this activity and create a game that uses phrases.

Between-station action: Girls use color chips and find things to match with each color as they travel to the next station.

Station 3: Yellow. "What holds the Scarecrow together?" World of the Out-of-Doors. "Knots" from "Outdoor Fun" (*Brownie Girl Scout Handbook*, page 237). Have the girls learn at least three knots.

Between-station action: Girls follow a trail laid with straw markers.

Station 4: Red. "What do you need for a healthy heart?" World of Well-Being. "Animal Moves" from "Dancercize" (*Brownie Girl Scout Handbook*, page 192). Girls do activities with leader.

Between-station action: Girls follow a tunnel and obstacle course trail made of large cardboard boxes to the next station.

Station 5: Purple. "Look, there's the Emerald City." World of the Arts. "The Best Neighborhood" from "Artful Architecture" (*Brownie Girl Scout Handbook*, page 175). Have the girls create a group collage of their ideal neighborhood after a discussion on what things they would like to include.

Between-station action: Follow a trail laid with stone trail signs.

Station 6: Green. "Green stands for Girl Scouts, and they have fun!" Have each group develop a cheer about its group name.

Between-station action: Play follow-the-leader to the next station.

Directions for each group after it has arrived back at the first station:

Each group receives sealed orders to return to a central gathering place, where they rejoin the circle and sing "Make New Friends" after closing comments. Ask each girl to think about a new friend she has made as the friendship squeeze is passed around the friendship circle.

GIRL SCOUT PROGRAM LINKS

The Guide For Daisy Girl Scout Leaders

Brownie Girl Scout Handbook (1993 Ed.)

The World of Well-Being:
    Caring for Children
    Health and Fitness
    Healthy Relationships
    Sports
    Sports Sampler
The World of People:
    Creative Solutions
    Girl Scouting Around the World
    My Heritage
Now and Then: Stories from Around the World
    The World in My Community
    Women's Stories
    World Neighbors
The World of the Arts:
    Toymaker
    Visual Arts
The World of Today and Tomorrow:
    Computer Fun
    Dabbler Badge
    Do-It-Yourself
    Math Whiz
    Plants and Animals
    Puzzlers
The World of the Out-of-Doors:
    Frosty Fun
    Horseback Rider
    Outdoor Fun
    Outdoor Fun in the City
    Water Fun

Cadette Girl Scout Handbook

Leadership, pages 38–42, 118, 131.
Healthy Living/Good Health in Action, pages 60–64.
Handling Stress, pages 88–90.
Exploring New Interests, pages 108–124.

Interest Projects for Cadette and Senior Girl Scouts (1997 Ed.)

Sports and Recreation:
    Backpacking
    Camping
    Games for Life
    High Adventure
    Horse Sense
    On the Courts
    On the Playing Field
    Orienteering
    Paddle, Pole, and Roll
    Rolling Along
    Smooth Sailing
    Sports for Life
    Water Sports

A Resource Book for Senior Girl Scouts

Leadership, pages 16, 65–92.
Health and Well Being, pages 29–64.
Stress Reducers, page 61.
Recreational Activities, pages 127–132.

Leadership Projects for Cadette and Senior Girl Scouts

Leader-in-Training/Counselor-in-Training Core Course Design.
Getting Acquainted/Introductions (Session 1), pages 24–25.
Leadership Skills (Session 5), pages 30–31.

RESOURCES FOR LEADERS AND GIRLS

Barry, Sheila A. *The World's Best Travel Games.* New York: Sterling Publishing Co., 1988. Includes games for different modes of transportation, waiting, and eating out.

Cornell, Joseph Bharat. *Sharing Nature with Children: A Parent's and Teacher's Nature Awareness Guidebook.* Nevada City, Calif: Ananda Publications, 1979. A pocketbook of nature games and activities that can be played outdoors anytime with all ages. Great for a day pack.

Fleming, June. *Games (and More!) for Backpackers.* New York: Perigee Books, Putnam Publishing Group, 1979. A great book for field trips and backpacking. It is light enough to take along.

Fletcher, Ruth. *Teaching Peace: Skills for Living in a Global Society.* San Francisco, Calif.: Harper & Row, 1986. An excellent source for simulation gaming on a global scale, as well as activities that look at conflict resolution, prejudice, stereotyping, disabilities, cooperation, and distribution of resources.

Fluegelman, Andrew, ed. *The New Games Book.* New Games Foundation. San Francisco, Calif.: Headlands Press, 1976. The original "play hard, play fair, nobody hurt" games book for all ages, all-size groups. An excellent resource.

Fluegelman, Andrew. *More New Games!* San Francisco, Calif.: Headlands Press, 1981. More new games, along with a good explanation of new games philosophy. For all ages.

Goodman, Joel, and Matt Weinstein. *Playfair: Everybody's Guide to Noncompetitive Play.* San Luis Obispo, Calif.: Impact Publishers, 1980. Emphasis on noncompetitive fun games. The chapters on mixers, energizers, and leadership training are very helpful for older girls and adult leader trainings.

Grunfeld, Frederick V. *Games of the World—How to Make Them, How to Play Them, How They Came to Be.* Swiss Committee for Unicef, Zurich. New York: Plenary Publications International, Inc., 1975. A beautifully illustrated game book for all ages from around the world. Illustrates the love of games that we all share.

Henderson, Roxanne. *The Picture Rulebook of Kids' Games.* Chicago: Contemporary Books, Inc., 1996. Good selection of games, especially sections on sidewalk and ball games. Simple, effective illustrations. Screen for safety.

Houston, Kathleen M., and Nancy V. Speakman. *Wide Games: Activities for Large Groups.* Outdoor Adventure Enterprises, 1982. Written by professional Girl Scouts, this book shows how to develop wide games and presents a number of them for use.

Hoxie, W. J. *How Girls Can Help Their Country.* New York: Girl Scouts of the U.S.A., 1913, 1972. A chapter on games contains some gems girls might enjoy for comparison. Discuss safety beforehand. Available in most council libraries.

Hurwitz, Abraham, and Manny Sternlicht. *Games Children Play: Instructive and Creative Play Activities for the Mentally Retarded and Developmentally Disabled Child.* New York: Van Nostrand Reinhold Company, 1981. Presents games for specific developmental stimulation in working with children with disabilities. Many sensory games.

LeFevre, Dale N. *New Games for the Whole Family*. New York: Perigee Books, the Putnam Publishing Group, 1988. These are new games that have been played around the world with all ages. There's even a chapter entitled "Games for Your Bomb Shelter," perfect for those inclement weather camp outs. An excellent and engaging resource.

Maguire, Jack. *Hopscotch, Hot Potato, Ha Ha Ha—A Rulebook of Children's Games*. New York: Simon and Schuster, 1990. Excellent index by age and type. Includes water and party games.

Orlick, Terry. *The Cooperative Sports and Games Book: Challenge Without Competition*. New York: Pantheon Books, 1978. Emphasis on cooperative games in which "everyone cooperates, everybody wins, and nobody loses." Games for ages 3–7, 8–12. Good educational rationale for games and a chapter on creating your own games.

Pearse, Jack. *Clouds on the Clothesline and 200 Other Great Games*. Ontario, Canada: Cober Printing Ltd., 1981, 1986. A good resource for any camp counselor's library, and one that covers all situations.

Pearse, Jack. *Lead On . . . Counselor*. Ontario, Canada: Cober Printing Ltd., 1982. Includes a good selection of games and large group activities for a camp environment.

Rice, Wayne, and Mike Yaconelli. *Creative Socials and Special Events*. Grand Rapids, Mich.: Youth Specialties, Zonervan Publishing House, 1986. This is geared for teens and teen youth group (church) events, and has a lot of good ideas. Older girls might find it fun to use as a resource for planning special events. (Useful for older Junior Girl Scouts as well.)

Rice, Wayne, and Mike Yaconelli. *Play It! Great Games for Groups*. Grand Rapids, Mich.: Youth Specialties, Zonervan Publishing House, 1986. An excellent source for group games for any occasion. Chapter on wide games presents group games that require more space and strategies.

Salter, Richard. *"Are We There Yet?"* Travel Games for Kids. New York, N.Y.: Prince Paperback, Crown Publishers, 1991. A wonderful resource for on the road travel games, whether going by car, bus, or plane.

The Usborne Book of Games and Puzzles. London: Usborne Publishing Ltd., 1994. Colorful, well illustrated games to make and play. Includes board games and quizzes as well.

INDEX

Indoor

Outdoor

Either

Small Group

Large Group

Either (group)

International in Origin

Younger Girls

Older Girls

All Ages